AF422625

UNBELIEVABLE SHORT STORIES FOR SENIORS

FOR SENIORS

172 OF THE MOST EXTRAORDINARY STORIES FROM

WORLD HISTORY AND POP CULTURE

ALBERT CHESTER

Copyright © 2023 by Albert Chester

All rights reserved, the content contained within this book may not be reproduced, duplicated or transmitted without direct written permission from the author or the publisher.

Under no circumstances will any blame or legal responsibility be held against the publisher, or author, for any damages, reparation, or monetary loss due to the information contained within this book, either directly or indirectly.

Please note the information contained within this document is for educational and entertainment purposes only. All effort has been executed to present accurate, up to date, reliable, complete information. No warranties of any kind are declared or implied. Readers acknowledge that the author is not engaged in the rendering of legal, medical or professional advice. The content within this book has been derived from various sources. Please consult a licensed professional before attempting any techniques outlined in this book.

By reading this document, the reader agrees that under no circumstances is the author responsible for any losses, direct or indirect, that are incurred as a result of the use of the information contained within this document, including, but not limited to, errors, omissions, or inaccuracies.

AMERICA'S FIRST AND LAST EMPEROR

September 17, 1859

Emperor Joshua Norton was a unique and memorable figure in San Francisco history, who lived during the mid-19th century. Born in England in 1819, he immigrated to South Africa and later to San Francisco, where he made a fortune as a commission merchant and later lost it all due to failed investments. Despite his financial struggles, Norton did not let this bring him down and instead decided to declare himself "Emperor of These United States" and "Protector of Mexico" in 1859.

His imperial decrees, issued on official-looking stationery, were both serious and comical. For example, he demanded the abolition of the U.S. Congress and called for the construction of a bridge connecting San Francisco to Oakland. Despite the lack of actual authority behind these declarations, Emperor Norton was taken seriously by the citizens of San Francisco, who saw him as a harmless and charming eccentric. He was known to parade around the city in his imperial regalia, which included a blue uniform with gold braid, a beaver hat, and a sword.

Emperor Norton was widely respected and even celebrated by the people of San Francisco. Local businesses honored his imperial currency, and restaurants set a place for him at the head table. He was often seen taking walks around the city and was even invited to give speeches and attend events. Despite his imperial title, Emperor Norton lived in poverty, relying on the generosity of the citizens of San Francisco to provide for his basic needs.

In 1880, Emperor Norton passed away, and his funeral was a grand affair attended by thousands of mourners who wished to pay their respects to this unique and beloved figure. To this day, he remains an important part of San Francisco history, celebrated as a symbol of the city's quirky and eccentric spirit. His life and legacy continue to inspire residents and visitors alike, who see him as a reminder that the world is full of surprises and that anything is possible.

A WAR STARTED OVER A STOLEN BUCKET

January, 1325

The War of the Bucket, also known as the Guelphs and Ghibellines War, was a conflict between the city-states of Bologna and Modena in Italy that took place in 1325. The war was initiated by a seemingly trivial matter, a stolen bucket, but its underlying cause was rooted in the political and power struggles between the city-states of northern Italy during the Middle Ages.

The bucket in question was a wooden bucket used to draw water from a well in Bologna. According to the legend, a group of Modenese soldiers stole the bucket as a prank, causing great offense to the people of Bologna. In response, the Bolognese declared war on Modena and mobilized their army. The war lasted for several months and involved several battles and skirmishes between the two cities. The conflict was intense, with both sides suffering significant losses, but in the end, Bologna emerged victorious.

The War of the Bucket had far-reaching consequences beyond the two cities involved. It marked the beginning of the conflict between the Guelphs and Ghibellines, two opposing factions in medieval Italy that represented the struggle between the Papacy and the Holy Roman Empire. The conflict also demonstrated the growing militarization of the city-states of northern Italy and the increasing tensions between them.

The War of the Bucket is remembered as one of the most absurd and humorous wars in European history. Nevertheless, it serves as an important reminder of the dangers of power struggles and the need for peaceful resolution of conflicts. The bucket that started the war was returned to Bologna as a symbol of their victory and became a source of pride for the city. To this day, the bucket is displayed in the town square as a reminder of the city's rich history and the power of symbols in shaping the course of events.

A POPE PUT HIS DEAD PREDECESSOR ON TRIAL

Year 897

The Cadaver Synod, also known as the Synod of the Corpses, was a macabre and bizarre event in the history of the Roman Catholic Church that took place in the year 897. The synod was held in Rome and was presided over by Pope Stephen VI. At the time, Pope Stephen was locked in a power struggle with his predecessor, Pope Formosus, who had died a few months prior. Pope Stephen, who was seen as a puppet of the powerful Roman aristocracy, saw Pope Formosus as a threat to his authority and wanted to discredit him.

To achieve this, Pope Stephen ordered that Pope Formosus's body be exhumed and put on trial. The dead pope was dressed in his papal vestments and placed on a throne in the Basilica of St. John Lateran. Pope Stephen then presided over the trial, which was a sham, as the deceased Pope Formosus could not defend himself. Pope Stephen charged Pope Formosus with various crimes, including the acts of violating church law by accepting the papacy while he was still a bishop, and performing ordinations without proper authorization. Despite the absurdity of the charges, the synod found Pope Formosus guilty and declared his ordinations invalid.

The synod also ordered that Pope Formosus's body be stripped of its papal vestments, three fingers used for blessings to be cut off, and the body to be thrown into the Tiber River. The synod's decision was met with widespread outrage and was seen as a direct challenge to the authority of the papacy.

Pope Stephen's actions were soon overturned by his successor, Pope Theodore II, who declared the synod and its verdict null and void. Pope Formosus's body was retrieved from the Tiber River and reinterred with honor in St. Peter's Basilica. The Cadaver Synod remains a shocking and gruesome episode in the history of the Catholic Church, a testament to the power struggles and political maneuvering that have taken place within the church throughout its history.

ALBERT EINSTEIN'S BRAIN WAS STOLEN AND MISSING FOR DECADES

April 18, 1955

The story of Albert Einstein's brain is a well-known and intriguing episode in the history of science and medicine. After his death on April 18, 1955, Einstein's body was autopsied at Princeton Hospital, and the pathologist on duty, Dr. Thomas Harvey, made the controversial decision to remove Einstein's brain for further study. Dr. Harvey believed that the study of Einstein's brain would reveal the secrets of the genius mind and wanted to preserve it for scientific research.

However, Dr. Harvey's actions were not in line with the established protocols for handling human brains used for scientific research. He did not properly preserve the brain, instead storing it in jars, in his office, and then in his basement for several years. Additionally, he did not seek the consent of Einstein's family or obtain a scientific grant for research, raising ethical concerns about the removal and study of human brains.

For several decades, the whereabouts of Einstein's brain were largely unknown. Rumors circulated about its location, but it was not until 1978 that it was discovered that Harvey still had the brain in his possession.

Eventually, the brain was studied by a number of scientists, who discovered several interesting findings. For instance, Einstein's brain had a larger than average prefrontal cortex, which is associated with abstract reasoning and problem-solving abilities. This observation supports the theory that the exceptional abilities of genius minds, such as Einstein's, are related to differences in brain structure and function.

In addition to these findings, the story of Albert Einstein's brain also highlights important ethical questions about the study of human brains and the need for informed consent and proper protocols. Despite its controversial nature, the story of Einstein's brain remains an important part of scientific history and continues to inspire research into the human brain and the nature of genius.

5,000 SOUTHERNERS FLED TO BRAZIL POST-CIVIL WAR

April 9, 1865

After the American Civil War, a small number of Southern sympathizers and Confederate veterans emigrated to Brazil to escape the aftermath of the conflict and start anew. Some of these emigrants established communities in Brazil and formed groups that sought to maintain Southern culture and traditions.

One of the largest and most well-known of these communities was established in the state of São Paulo, where the Confederate expatriates purchased a large plot of land and established a colony known as Americana. In Americana, the Southerners built homes, churches, schools, and other institutions that reflected their Southern heritage. They also sought to maintain the Confederate ideology, and some of the leaders of the community continued to promote the principles of the Confederacy even decades after the Civil War.

However, despite their efforts, the Southern communities in Brazil faced numerous challenges and difficulties. Many of the emigrants struggled to adapt to the new environment and culture, and some suffered from homesickness. Additionally, they encountered financial difficulties, as they had limited resources and the Brazilian economy was not as developed as they had hoped.

Despite these challenges, some of the Southern communities in Brazil managed to survive and even thrive for several decades. The descendants of the Confederate emigrants continued to maintain their Southern heritage and traditions, and some still carry on the legacy of the Confederacy today.

Overall, the story of the Confederate emigrants in Brazil is a fascinating chapter in the history of the American South and a testament to the resilience and determination of those who sought to maintain their cultural identity and traditions in the face of adversity.

THE MOST KISSED GIRL IN THE WORLD

Mid-1960s

The "most kissed girl in the world" is a nickname that has been attached to the story of Anita Collins, a young woman who tragically drowned in a boating accident in the mid-1960s. Following her death, her parents consented to the use of her head mold for the creation of a CPR training dummy. The dummy, known as the "Resusci Anne" CPR training manikin, was manufactured by the Norwegian company Asmund Laerdal and has been used for CPR training since its introduction in the 1960s.

The Resusci Anne manikin has since become one of the most widely used CPR training dummies in the world and is used in CPR training courses by organizations, institutions, and medical professionals globally. The image of the manikin's face, based on Collins' mold, has become synonymous with CPR training, and the manikin is credited with playing a crucial role in saving countless lives through CPR training exercises.

In recognition of its impact and widespread use, the Resusci Anne manikin has received numerous accolades, including being inducted into the Medical Museum Hall of Fame in Washington, D.C. Moreover, the manikin has undergone numerous updates and advancements over the years to reflect the latest CPR techniques and recommendations.

Despite the nickname, the story of Anita Collins serves as a reminder of the importance of CPR training and the role it plays in saving lives. Her legacy lives on through the continued use of the CPR training manikin and the lives it has helped to save. The "most kissed girl in the world" nickname is a testament to the impact and significance of the CPR training manikin in the field of medicine and health.

THE CIA DISCUSSED KILLING FIDEL CASTRO WITH AND EXPLODING CIGAR

Unknown Date

The alleged plot to assassinate Fidel Castro, the former Cuban leader, using an exploding cigar is one of the most famous and disputed stories of the Cold War era. The United States government, particularly the Central Intelligence Agency (CIA), has been accused of attempting to kill Castro on numerous occasions.

According to multiple sources, the CIA was said to have developed a plan to give Castro an exploding cigar, which would detonate when he lit it and kill him. However, there is limited and often conflicting evidence to support this claim, and the CIA has not officially acknowledged any involvement in the matter.

It's important to note that the U.S. government has a long history of employing covert operations and propaganda to influence foreign countries, and information regarding such operations is often classified and kept confidential. As a result, the truth about the exploding cigar plot may never be fully known.

Despite the lack of concrete evidence, the story of the exploding cigar has become a well-known part of popular culture and a symbol of the political tensions and secret operations of the Cold War. While some experts believe it to be an urban legend, others believe it to be a genuine attempt by the CIA to kill Castro. However, without official confirmation from the U.S. government or the CIA, it remains a topic of speculation and debate.

FRANZ FERDINAND DODGED AN ASSASSIN ATTEMPT WITH A TWIST

June 28, 1914

The assassination of Archduke Franz Ferdinand of Austria-Hungary on June 28, 1914, is widely considered as the spark that ignited the First World War. The Archduke, who was the heir to the Austro-Hungarian Empire, was on a visit to Sarajevo, Bosnia, when he and his wife, Sophie, were assassinated by Gavrilo Princip, a member of a Serbian nationalist organization called the Black Hand.

Prior to the fateful encounter with Princip, the Archduke and his wife actually escaped an assassination attempt earlier in the day. During a drive through the streets of Sarajevo, a bomb was thrown at their car by another member of the Black Hand, but it bounced off the car and exploded under the following vehicle, injuring several people but leaving the Archduke unharmed.

However, the Archduke and his wife's luck ran out when they decided to visit the wounded from the bomb attack at a hospital. Due to a miscommunication, the couple's driver took a wrong turn and ended up at a café, where they encountered Princip, who was waiting on the sidewalk. The assassin took advantage of the opportunity and shot the Archduke and his wife at close range, killing them both.

The assassination of Archduke Franz Ferdinand was a critical moment in history, as it set off a chain of events that ultimately led to the outbreak of World War I. The Austro-Hungarian Empire declared war on Serbia, which sparked a series of alliances and declarations of war, eventually leading to a global conflict. The incident has been studied extensively by historians and is considered one of the most significant events of the 20th century, as it resulted in the loss of millions of lives and the reshaping of the political and economic landscape of the world.

FALSE MILITARY ALARM IN LOS ANGELES

February 25, 1942

On February 25, 1942, the city of Los Angeles was thrown into a state of alarm and confusion when it was believed that the city was under attack from enemy forces. At the time, the threat of a Japanese attack on the West Coast was very real, as the United States had recently entered World War II following the bombing of Pearl Harbor.

That evening, Army anti-aircraft artillery batteries detected an unidentified aircraft over the city, and in response, launched a barrage of anti-aircraft fire and activated searchlights, creating a dramatic display in the sky. Sirens blared throughout the city, sending residents running for cover and adding to the chaos. The anti-aircraft barrage lasted for over an hour, with over 1,400 rounds of ammunition being fired, but the aircraft turned out to be a weather balloon, not an enemy bomber.

The "Great Los Angeles Air Raid" caused widespread panic, with many residents reportedly taking to the streets in fear and some even evacuating the city. Despite the lack of actual enemy presence, the incident had lasting effects on the city and its residents, highlighting the power of fear and misinformation. The event also served as a reminder of the United States' military readiness and demonstrated the country's preparedness to defend itself against potential threats.

In the aftermath of the event, it was discovered that the anti-aircraft batteries had misidentified the weather balloon and the searchlights had been activated due to a communication error between military personnel. The incident was widely reported in the media and has since become a part of the cultural history of Los Angeles and the United States. It serves as a cautionary tale, reminding us of the dangers of fear and misinformation and the importance of accurate communication and military readiness.

E.T. VIDEO GAME SO BAD IT HAD TO BE BURIED

September, 1982

The story of the E.T. the Extra-Terrestrial video game is widely considered to be one of the biggest commercial failures in the history of the gaming industry. In 1982, the video game company Atari secured the rights to create a video game based on the highly popular movie "E.T. the Extra-Terrestrial." However, the company was under pressure to release the game in time for the holiday season, which led to the game being rushed through the development process.

The E.T. video game was released in September 1982, but it was widely criticized for its poor gameplay, confusing controls, and low-quality graphics. The game received negative reviews from both gamers and critics, and it failed to sell well in stores. Despite high expectations, the game only sold an estimated 1.5 million units, far short of Atari's projected sales of 5 million units.

Due to the game's commercial failure, Atari was left with millions of unsold copies of the E.T. game. To dispose of these surplus cartridges, the company reportedly buried them in a landfill site in Alamogordo, New Mexico, along with other surplus hardware and outdated video games. This event became a legend in the gaming world and is often cited as one of the factors that contributed to the North American video game crash of 1983.

In 2014, the landfill site was excavated by a team of documentary filmmakers, who discovered thousands of E.T. cartridges, along with other Atari products, buried in the landfill. This excavation confirmed the truth of the story and served as a reminder of the importance of quality control in the gaming industry.

In conclusion, the E.T. the Extra-Terrestrial video game is an important cautionary tale in the history of the gaming industry. The game's commercial failure and subsequent burial of thousands of unsold cartridges serve as a warning about the dangers of rushing a product to market without proper development and testing, as well as the importance of delivering a high-quality product to the consumer.

BENJAMIN FRANKLIN ELECTROCUTED HIMSELF, BUT NOT WITH HIS KITE

1752

Benjamin Franklin is a legendary figure in the history of science and is widely known for his famous kite experiment, which demonstrated the electrical nature of lightning. However, not many people are aware of another incident involving Benjamin Franklin and electricity that took place outside of his kite experiment.

According to historical records, Benjamin Franklin was a passionate experimenter who loved to explore the properties of electricity in his own home. He was known to conduct various electrical experiments using metal chains and other conductive materials. On one occasion, during one of these experiments, Franklin accidentally touched an electrified metal chain and received a shock. Despite the intensity of the shock, he was able to recover quickly and continue his experiments without any long-term effects.

This incident highlights the dangers of conducting electrical experiments without proper safety precautions, especially during a time when the understanding of electricity was still in its early stages. Despite the risks, Benjamin Franklin continued to be driven by his curiosity and passion for electricity. He went on to make significant contributions to the field, including the discovery of positive and negative charges, the development of the lightning rod, and the creation of the first battery.

In conclusion, while Benjamin Franklin is most famous for his kite experiment, he also had another, lesser-known incident involving electricity that took place during his experiments at home. This incident serves as a reminder of the importance of conducting scientific experiments with caution and care, especially when working with potentially dangerous materials, and underscores the passion and dedication that drove Benjamin Franklin to push the boundaries of scientific knowledge.

THE UNSOLVED AXE MURDERER

1912

The Villisca axe murder was a brutal and gruesome crime that occurred in the small town of Villisca, Iowa, in the United States on June 10, 1912. On that fateful night, six members of the Moore family, including four children, and two guests were found murdered in their home with an axe.

The Moore family, consisting of Josiah Moore, his wife Sarah, their children Herman, Katherine, Boyd, and Paul, and two guests, Lena and Ina Stillinger, were all found bludgeoned to death in their beds. The crime scene was incredibly brutal and the evidence suggested that the murderer had used an axe to commit the murders.

The investigation into the Villisca axe murders was extensive, but despite numerous suspects and arrests, the case was never officially solved. Over the years, several theories have been put forth as to who committed the murders, but none have been definitively proven.

One of the most prominent theories is that a traveling minister named Reverend George Kelly was responsible for the killings. Kelly was in Villisca on the night of the murders and was known to have a history of mental instability. Despite the circumstantial evidence against him, Kelly was never formally charged with the crimes and always maintained his innocence.

Another theory implicates a local man named Andy Sawyer, who was known to have had a contentious relationship with the Moore family. However, like Kelly, Sawyer was never formally charged with the crimes and also always maintained his innocence.

The Villisca axe murders remain one of the most notorious and puzzling unsolved crimes in American history. To this day, the case continues to captivate the public imagination and spark numerous debates about who the true killer was and why they committed such a horrific crime.

EMPEROR NERO ON KILLING HIS OWN MOTHER

54-68 AD

The story of Nero's alleged attempt to kill his mother, Agrippina the Younger, is a well-known historical account from ancient Rome. According to the ancient historian Tacitus, Nero was known for his cruelty and erratic behavior during his reign as Emperor of Rome from 54 to 68 AD. He was known for his tyrannical rule, as well as his extravagance, and his alleged attempt to kill his mother is often cited as an example of his cruel and unpredictable nature.

The story goes that Nero plotted to kill Agrippina by building a collapsing boat and inviting her to take a voyage on it. The boat was constructed in such a way that it was supposed to sink and kill Agrippina, but she reportedly survived and managed to swim to shore. When Nero found out that his plan had failed, he is said to have ordered her murder.

It's important to note that the accounts of Tacitus and other ancient historians can sometimes be biased and exaggerated, and there is often conflicting information about events and personalities from this time period. Therefore, it's difficult to determine the true facts about this specific incident and to what extent it may have actually happened.

However, Nero's relationship with his mother was famously tumultuous, and the stories about their interactions, whether factual or not, serve as a reminder of the power struggles and familial conflicts that existed in ancient Rome. Nero is said to have had a strained relationship with his mother, who was known for her ambition and desire for power. The alleged attempt to kill her is often seen as a result of her attempts to exert influence over Nero and his rule.

In conclusion, while the story of Nero's alleged attempt to kill his mother may not be entirely accurate, it serves as an example of the infamous reputation Nero had during his reign as Emperor of Rome. The story of their turbulent relationship also highlights the power struggles and familial conflicts that existed in ancient Rome during this time.

POSTHUMOUS EXECUTIONS BY KING CHARLES II

1660

King Charles II was the son of King Charles I, who was executed in 1649 after a long and bloody civil war between the Royalists and the Parliamentarians. After his father's execution, Charles II spent nine years in exile in Europe before returning to England as part of a military expedition led by General George Monck.

Upon his return, Charles II was welcomed by many as the rightful king and was crowned at Westminster Abbey in 1661. He faced numerous challenges during his reign, including the Great Plague of 1665 and the Great Fire of London in 1666, as well as opposition from those who opposed his religious and political views.

However, one of the most infamous events of Charles II's reign was his ordering of posthumous executions. This occurred after the failed Rye House Plot to overthrow him. Despite the conspirators having already suffered the consequences of their actions, Charles ordered their execution, including disinterring their bodies and putting them on public display. This act was widely criticized and is considered a dark moment in his reign, as it was seen as a violation of the principle of double jeopardy and a sign of his cruelty and disregard for the rule of law.

Despite this, Charles II remains an important figure in English history, known for his role in restoring the monarchy after the Commonwealth period, his contributions to the arts and sciences, and his love of pleasure and entertainment. He is remembered as the "Merry Monarch."

WW2 JAPANESE SOLIDERS DIDN'T KNOW THE WAS ENDED UNTIL 1970

1970s

In the 1970s, reports emerged of Japanese soldiers who were still unaware that World War 2 had ended. These soldiers were located in remote islands in the Pacific and had been cut off from communication with the outside world for decades.

According to the reports, these soldiers continued to live as though the war was still ongoing and remained loyal to the Emperor of Japan. They had been stationed on these islands during the war and were never informed of Japan's surrender in 1945. Over the years, many of their fellow soldiers had passed away, leaving only a small number behind to carry on the belief that the war was still raging.

The Japanese government was slow to acknowledge these reports, but eventually sent a delegation to the islands to verify them. When the delegation arrived, they found that the soldiers were indeed living in a state of unawareness and had continued to follow their military routines and duties.

The delegation carefully approached the soldiers and informed them that the war had ended and that Japan had surrendered. Many of the soldiers were shocked and struggled to come to terms with the news. Some were reluctant to believe it and continued to live as they had before, while others decided to return to mainland Japan to reintegrate into society.

The story of these Japanese soldiers serves as a reminder of the lasting impact of war and the importance of keeping lines of communication open during times of conflict. It is also a testament to the bravery and loyalty of the soldiers who continued to carry out their duties, even when they had been forgotten by the world.

TOP HAT'S FIRST APPEARANCE WAS CONTROVERSIAL

January, 1797

The exact origin of the top hat is uncertain, but it is widely believed to have been popularized in the late 18th and early 19th centuries by a man named John Hetherington. Hetherington was a hatter by trade, and in January of 1797, he caused a stir in the streets of London by wearing a top hat for the first time in public.

At the time, hats were an important symbol of social status, and the traditional hat of the day was the tricorne, a low-crowned, wide-brimmed hat that was often decorated with feathers or ribbons. Hetherington's top hat, in contrast, was tall, cylindrical, and made of silk, with a narrow brim and no decorations.

When Hetherington stepped out onto the streets wearing his new hat, onlookers were reportedly shocked. Some people were said to have been frightened by the strange and unfamiliar headwear, while others were amused or amazed. The incident quickly became the talk of the town, and Hetherington's hat was widely imitated in the following months and years, eventually becoming a symbol of the fashionable and wealthy.

Despite its initial controversy, the top hat went on to become one of the most iconic and enduring styles of headwear in history. It has been worn by countless famous figures over the years, including Abraham Lincoln, Winston Churchill, and Fred Astaire, and remains an enduring symbol of elegance and sophistication.

CATHOLICS AND PROTESTANTS THROWN OUT OF WINDOWS

1618

The political dispute between Catholics and Protestants in 1618 was not the first time that tensions between the two groups had boiled over in the city of Prague. Nearly 200 years earlier, in 1419, a similar conflict had arisen, and this time it was the Catholics who were on the offensive. During the First Defenestration of Prague, a group of radical Catholics threw seven members of the Prague city council out of a window in the New Town Hall, following a power struggle between the council and the Catholic Church. The incident was a turning point in the history of the city and led to increased tensions between the Catholics and the followers of the Hussite movement, a precursor to the Protestant Reformation.

Fast forward to 1618, and the political dispute between Catholics and Protestants had once again come to a head. The Catholic Habsburg dynasty was determined to stamp out Protestantism, and tensions between the two groups were at an all-time high.

In May 1618, three Catholic regents were thrown out of a window in the royal palace in Prague, in an event known as the Second Defenestration of Prague. This incident was seen as a turning point in the conflict, and it quickly escalated into the Thirty Years' War, one of the deadliest and most destructive conflicts in European history. The Thirty Years' War lasted from 1618 to 1648, and it resulted in the deaths of millions of people and widespread devastation and economic disruption. The war ultimately led to the Treaty of Westphalia, which ended the conflict and recognized the independence of the Protestant states. The treaty also recognized the principle of cuius regio, eius religio, which allowed each ruler to choose the religion of their own territory, and marked a turning point in European history by establishing the concept of religious tolerance.

The Defenestrations of Prague, both in 1419 and in 1618, serve as reminders of the deep-seated tensions that existed between Catholics and Protestants and the lengths to which people were willing to go to defend their beliefs.

THE DANCING PLAGUE OF 1518

1518

The "Dancing Plague" of 1518 was a phenomenon that occurred in the city of Strasbourg in Alsace (modern-day France). The outbreak began in July of that year, when a woman named Frau Troffea suddenly began dancing uncontrollably in the street. Within a week, over 30 other people had joined her, dancing erratically and without rest. The dance frenzy soon spread to hundreds of people and lasted for several days, causing many of the dancers to collapse from exhaustion, dehydration, and heart attack.

The dancing mania lasted for several months, and it was estimated that hundreds of people were affected. The phenomenon was widely reported throughout Europe and became known as the "Dancing Plague." Some reports indicate that the dancers would dance for days on end, with no apparent reason for stopping.

There are several theories about what caused the dancing mania. Some believe it was a form of mass hysteria, triggered by a combination of religious fervor, stress, and social conditions of the time. Others have suggested that the dancers were suffering from a kind of mass psychogenic illness, brought on by the collective stress and anxiety of the population. Some even speculated that the dancing was caused by a supernatural force or the influence of evil spirits.

Despite the efforts of physicians and church officials to stop the dancing, it continued for several months until it eventually died down. Many of the people affected by the dancing mania never fully recovered and suffered from permanent physical and mental disabilities.

The "Dancing Plague" of 1518 remains one of the most mysterious and unexplained events in history, and its causes continue to be debated by historians and scientists. Nevertheless, it serves as a fascinating and eerie example of how mass psychogenic illness can affect large populations.

1904 SUMMER OLYMPICS CONTROVERSY

1904

The 1904 Summer Olympics marathon is a well-known and controversial story in Olympic history. The event, which took place in St. Louis, Missouri, was the first time the marathon was included in the Summer Olympics. The marathon was won by American runner Thomas Hicks, but the controversy surrounding the race centered on the methods used to keep Hicks going and how he was able to cross the finish line.

During the race, Hicks began to suffer from exhaustion and dehydration. His handlers, who were following the race in a support vehicle, gave him strychnine, a highly toxic stimulant, and brandy to try to keep him going. Despite being in a state of delirium, Hicks was able to complete the race, but he required medical attention after crossing the finish line.

The use of performance-enhancing drugs was not against the rules of the 1904 Summer Olympics, and Hicks was not disqualified for his actions. However, the controversy surrounding the methods used to keep him going has called into question the integrity of the race and the victory of Hicks.

In the years since the 1904 Summer Olympics, the use of performance-enhancing drugs has become strictly prohibited, and stricter rules and regulations have been put in place to prevent such incidents from happening again. The story of the 1904 Summer Olympics marathon remains a controversial and often discussed topic in Olympic history, as it raises important questions about the balance between fair competition and the use of performance-enhancing methods.

PEARL HARBOR HERO MISSION

March 10, 1942

On March 10, 1942, just over three months after the attack on Pearl Harbor, Allied forces, primarily consisting of American and British troops, were forced to abandon Java Island in the Dutch East Indies (present-day Indonesia) during World War II. The Japanese had launched a massive invasion of the island and were quickly advancing, overwhelming the Allied forces. One remarkable moment during the evacuation was when Sergeant Harry Hayes, a skilled aircraft mechanic, stepped up to the plate. A B-17 bomber had been damaged in the intense fighting, and the crew had been forced to abandon the plane. But Sergeant Hayes, determined to get the plane flying again, worked tirelessly to repair it. His efforts paid off, as he was not only able to get the bomber back in the air but also, to everyone's surprise, he successfully piloted the bomber, along with 17 other Americans, to Australia. Despite having no prior flight training, Sergeant Hayes successfully navigated the plane, flying by the seat of his pants and relying on his instincts. To make matters even more challenging, he did not have access to maps or instruments, making the journey even more treacherous. Yet, he was able to guide the plane to safety and deliver the passengers to Australia. Faced with the choice of being captured or potentially facing a massacre, the Allies made the difficult decision to evacuate as many troops as possible. They embarked on a perilous journey, facing many challenges such as limited resources, intense fighting, and challenging weather conditions. Many soldiers were left behind, either because they were injured or because there were not enough ships to evacuate everyone. The evacuation from Java was a significant loss for the Allies and marked the beginning of a series of defeats in the Pacific War. It also had a profound impact on the soldiers who were forced to leave their comrades behind and endure the hardships of war. Despite the setbacks, the Allies continued to fight and eventually achieved victory over Japan. The story of the evacuation of Java, and the bravery and determination shown by Sergeant Harry Hayes in particular, serves as a reminder of the sacrifices made by soldiers during times of war and the bravery they showed in the face of adversity. Sergeant Hayes's remarkable feat of repairing and piloting the bomber to safety in the face of such adversity is a testament to the courage and resourcefulness of the soldiers who served during World War II.

JULIUS CAESAR WAS HELD CAPTIVE BY PIRATES WITH A TURN OF EVENTS

75 BC

In 75 BC, Caesar was serving as a military tribune in the province of Asia (modern-day Turkey). During this time, he was captured by Cilician pirates, who demanded a ransom of 20 talents of silver (equivalent to about 7,200 kg of silver) for his release.

Caesar was undaunted by his capture and refused to be intimidated by the pirates. He told them that he was a Roman citizen and that they would pay for their audacity. He even went so far as to write poetry and make fun of the pirates, telling them that he would have their heads once he was released.

The pirates, who initially thought they had captured a wealthy and influential Roman, were taken aback by Caesar's boldness and confidence. They soon realized that they had underestimated their captive, who was not only wealthy, but also a well-connected and powerful figure in Rome.

Despite their initial misgivings, the pirates agreed to release Caesar after they received the ransom, which was paid by his family and friends. However, they did not know that they had made a terrible mistake.

Once he was free, Caesar immediately set out to gather a fleet and an army to capture the pirates. He eventually caught them and brought them to Rome, where he had them crucified in a public display of his power and determination.

This episode became famous throughout the Roman Empire and cemented Caesar's reputation as a fearless and capable leader. It also demonstrated the power and reach of Rome, as well as the determination of its citizens to protect their own. The story of Caesar's captivity and release is often seen as a turning point in his career, and is considered to be a key event in his eventual rise to power.

A CANADIAN PRIME MINISTER BURGLARY

1995

The 1995 break-in at Sussex Drive refers to a burglary that took place at the residence of Canadian Prime Minister Jean Chrétien in Ottawa, Ontario, on February 13, 1995. The Chrétien family was not at home at the time of the break-in.

According to reports, two men broke into the prime minister's residence and ransacked several rooms, including the bedrooms of Chrétien and his wife, Aline. The intruders took several items, including jewelry, silverware, and a briefcase, and caused extensive damage to the property.

The break-in caused a major stir in the Canadian media and sparked widespread concern about the security of the prime minister and his family. The Royal Canadian Mounted Police (RCMP) launched an investigation into the break-in and several suspects were arrested and charged in connection with the crime.

Despite the widespread coverage of the incident, many details about the break-in remain unknown to this day. Some reports suggest that the intruders were seeking information about the prime minister and his family, while others believe that the break-in was a simple case of theft.

Regardless of the motivations behind the break-in, it was a major event in Canadian history and raised important questions about the security of high-level political officials in the country. The incident also underscored the need for increased measures to protect the safety and privacy of the prime minister and his family.

ISLAND SOVEREIGNTY DISPUTE BETWEEN CANADA AND DENMARK

1930

Hans Island is a small, uninhabited island located in the Arctic Ocean between Greenland, which is part of the Kingdom of Denmark, and Canada. Despite its small size and lack of resources, the ownership of Hans Island has been a source of controversy between the two countries for several decades.

The island was first claimed by Denmark in the early 1930s, but Canada has also claimed the island as part of its territory. The dispute has largely been a matter of principle, as neither country has any practical use for the island. However, the ownership of the island is closely tied to the ownership of the surrounding waters, and the ownership of Hans Island could potentially impact the countries' rights to explore and exploit any oil, gas or mineral resources that may be found in the area.

The dispute has been peaceful, and both countries have made diplomatic efforts to resolve the issue, including negotiating a treaty on the delimitation of their continental shelf. In 2005, the foreign ministers of Canada and Denmark agreed to "put aside" the dispute and work together on joint research and development projects in the area.

Despite this agreement, both countries continue to assert their claims to the island, with Canadian and Danish officials visiting the island on a regular basis to plant their national flags. The visits have been seen as a symbolic way for the two countries to assert their sovereignty over the island and demonstrate their commitment to their respective claims.

In conclusion, the dispute over Hans Island is a minor international dispute, but it highlights the importance of sovereignty and territorial claims in the Arctic, as the region becomes increasingly important due to climate change and the potential for natural resources.

THE CHRISTMAS TRUCE OF WORLD WAR I

December 25, 1914

The Christmas Truce of 1914 during World War I is a well-known and beloved story that has become synonymous with the holiday season. The story goes that on Christmas Eve and Christmas Day, soldiers from opposing sides of the conflict spontaneously ceased fighting and instead, sang carols, played soccer games, and exchanged gifts.

This event is considered one of the most remarkable and unexpected moments of the war, and it has become a symbol of hope and humanity in the midst of a brutal and devastating conflict. The story has been passed down through the generations, and it is often retold as an example of the power of peace and the spirit of the holiday season.

It is true that a spontaneous and unofficial truce occurred along parts of the Western Front during Christmas of 1914, but the events of that day were much more complicated and nuanced than the simple story of soldiers putting down their weapons to exchange gifts and sing carols.

There is evidence that the Christmas Truce was not a widespread event, and it likely only occurred in specific areas along the front line. In some places, the fighting continued uninterrupted, and in other areas, there were only brief pauses in the hostilities. Moreover, the decisions to cease fighting were not always made by the soldiers themselves, but sometimes by higher-ranking officers.

In the end, the Christmas Truce was a temporary and fragile moment of peace in a brutal and devastating conflict. Although the cease-fire was eventually broken, the events of that day have become a symbol of hope and humanity in the midst of war, and they continue to inspire people around the world to work towards peace and understanding.

THE BATTLE OF TEUTOBURG

9 AD

The Battle of the Teutoburg Forest was a pivotal moment in ancient Germanic history, marked by the defeat of the Roman Empire by a coalition of Germanic tribes led by the chieftain Segimerus and his son Arminius. This battle took place in 9 AD, and its outcome had far-reaching consequences for both the Germanic peoples and the Roman Empire.

Segimerus was a prominent leader among the Cherusci, one of the Germanic tribes in the region that is now modern-day Germany. At the time, the Roman Empire had conquered and incorporated the region into its territories as the province of Germania. However, the Germanic tribes were often resentful of Roman rule, and Segimerus and his tribe were no exception.

In 9 AD, a Roman governor named Publius Quinctilius Varus was sent to quell a rebellion in the region. As Varus and his troops were making their way through the forested region, they were ambushed by Segimerus and his son Arminius, who had formed an alliance with other Germanic tribes.

The battle was a complete rout, with the Roman army being caught off guard and unable to defend itself effectively in the dense forest. The exact number of Roman casualties is not known, but it is estimated that as many as 20,000 soldiers may have died in the battle.

This victory marked a turning point in Germanic history, with Segimerus and Arminius being hailed as heroes among the Germanic tribes. The defeat of the Roman army was a major blow to the empire's prestige, and it marked the end of Roman expansion into Germania. The Battle of the Teutoburg Forest set the stage for further rebellions and uprisings by the Germanic tribes in the centuries to come, and it remains a powerful symbol of Germanic resistance against foreign domination to this day.

A TIDAL WAVE EXPLOSION OF MOLASSES

January 15, 1919

The Great Molasses Flood, also known as the Boston Molasses Disaster, was a tragic event that occurred in Boston, Massachusetts, on January 15, 1919. On that fateful day, a large storage tank filled with 2.3 million gallons of molasses burst, releasing a 25-foot-high wave of the sticky, viscous substance that flowed through the streets of the North End neighborhood at 35 miles per hour. The wave of molasses destroyed everything in its path, collapsing buildings, knocking houses off their foundations, and engulfing people, horses, and vehicles.

The disaster caused widespread destruction and loss of life. In total, 21 people died and over 150 others were injured. The cleanup effort took weeks and involved removing the thick layer of molasses that coated everything in the affected area. The aftermath of the disaster was felt for years, as the sickly sweet smell of the molasses lingered in the air and the syrup seeped into the soil and groundwater, contaminating wells and making the area uninhabitable for some time.

The cause of the disaster was found to be a combination of factors, including poor design and construction of the storage tank, a lack of proper maintenance and inspections, and substandard materials used in the tank's construction. The company responsible for the storage tank, United States Industrial Alcohol (USIA), was found to be negligent and was sued by the city of Boston. USIA eventually settled the lawsuit for $300,000, which was a substantial sum at the time.

The Great Molasses Flood remains one of the worst industrial disasters in American history, and it serves as a warning of the dangers of neglecting safety and maintenance in industrial operations. The disaster and its aftermath are still remembered in Boston, and the area where the disaster took place is now a park called Langone Park. A plaque there marks the spot where the tank once stood and serves as a memorial to the victims of the disaster.

PRESIDENT ANDREW JACKSON'S ASSASSINATION ATTEMPT

January 30, 1835

Richard Lawrence, a man who attempted to assassinate President Andrew Jackson on January 30, 1835.

Lawrence, who was an unemployed house painter, believed that he was the rightful King of England and that President Jackson was standing in his way. He snuck up behind Jackson while the President was leaving the Capitol building after a funeral and pulled out two pistols. Both pistols, however, failed to fire, even though they were in good working condition.

President Jackson, who was a former military man and known for his bravery, reacted quickly and started to fight Lawrence with his cane. Lawrence was eventually overpowered and arrested by Jackson's supporters.

Lawrence was put on trial and found not guilty by reason of insanity, becoming the first person to be acquitted in such a manner in the U.S. He was institutionalized and spent the rest of his life in mental institutions.

This event is a significant moment in American history and serves as a reminder of the sacrifices made by those who have held the office of the President of the United States.

NAPOLEON WINS OVER HIS ARMY WITH BRAVERY AND COURAGE

March 1815

The story about Napoleon Bonaparte exposing his chest to his army is a well-known moment from his legendary career. Napoleon was a French military leader and emperor who rose to prominence during the French Revolution and was known for his charisma, tactical genius, and daring leadership.

After being exiled to the island of Elba in 1814, Napoleon returned to France in March 1815, determined to reclaim his power. This marked the beginning of the "Hundred Days," a period of intense political and military activity in which Napoleon attempted to re-establish his rule over France.

As Napoleon traveled to Grenoble to meet with his army, he reportedly exposed his chest to the soldiers, challenging them to shoot him if they dared. This bold act of courage helped to rally his troops to his cause and allowed him to successfully march on Paris. With his army at his side, Napoleon was able to temporarily restore himself as the leader of France.

However, Napoleon's rule during the Hundred Days was short-lived. He was defeated at the Battle of Waterloo in June 1815, leading to his second and final exile, this time to the remote island of Saint Helena.

While the accuracy of the specific story about Napoleon exposing his chest to his army may be disputed, it remains a well-known moment in his legend and is often cited as an example of his fearless leadership and charisma. Regardless of the specifics, there is no denying that Napoleon was a remarkable historical figure who left a lasting impact on the world.

CROCODILE TROUBLE DURING WW2

1945

The Battle of Ramree Island, which took place during the Burma Campaign of World War II, was fought between British and Japanese forces in 1945. But what is most famous about the battle is not the military conflict itself, but rather the strange and often gruesome fate that befell some of the Japanese soldiers who tried to flee the island.

According to reports, a large number of Japanese soldiers attempted to escape the island by wading through a mangrove swamp, only to be attacked and devoured by saltwater crocodiles. Some estimates suggest that as many as 400 soldiers may have fallen prey to the huge reptiles.

This event has become the stuff of legend, with tales of the crocodiles dragging men underwater, their victims' screams echoing across the swamp. While some have disputed the veracity of these claims, the accounts of survivors and witnesses paint a picture of a truly terrifying ordeal.

It's unclear why so many crocodiles were present in the swamp or why they proved so aggressive, but it's possible that the soldiers' fleeing through the water stirred up the reptiles and provoked an attack. Regardless of the reasons, the events at Ramree Island remain a chilling reminder of the unexpected dangers that can arise even in the midst of a major military conflict.

It is important to note, however, that some experts have cast doubt on the scale of the crocodile attacks and the number of casualties. While there is no doubt that some Japanese soldiers met a gruesome end in the swamp, the actual number may have been exaggerated in the years since the battle. Nevertheless, the Battle of Ramree Island remains one of the most unusual and memorable events of World War II.

A DOG EXTINGIUSHED A BOMB BY PEEING ON IT

1944

Juliana was a Great Dane who lived during the tumultuous times of World War II. Born in a small village in England, she was taken in by a loving family who lived near the coast. Juliana quickly became a cherished member of the household and was known for her loyal and affectionate nature.

However, what set Juliana apart from other dogs was her incredible ability to sense when air raids were about to occur. Whenever she heard the sound of enemy planes approaching, she would bark loudly and persistently, warning everyone in the house to take cover in the air raid shelter. This continued to happen on a regular basis and soon, the entire village came to rely on Juliana's warning barks.

One fateful day, while playing in the backyard, Juliana noticed an incendiary bomb that had fallen from an enemy plane and landed in the grass. Without hesitation, she ran over to the bomb and started barking frantically. The family rushed outside, only to find that Juliana had discovered the bomb and was trying to protect everyone from it.

In that moment of crisis, Juliana did something truly remarkable. She lifted her leg and peed on the incendiary bomb, effectively putting out the fuse and preventing it from exploding. The family and the rest of the village were amazed at Juliana's bravery and quick thinking. As the war raged on, the number of air raids increased, and the people of the village relied more and more on Juliana's warning barks. She became a hero in the village, and her bravery and dedication to protecting her family and friends did not go unnoticed.

The Blue Cross Medal was a prestigious award given to animals that had shown exceptional bravery during times of war, and the family who lived with Juliana nominated her for this award. She was soon awarded the Blue Cross Medal for her bravery, quick thinking, and dedication to keeping the village safe during air raids.

THERE WERE FEMALE GLADIATORS IN ANCIENT ROME

1-200 AD

Female gladiators, known as gladiatrices, did exist in ancient Rome. Although they were not as common as male gladiators, they were a significant part of the history of gladiatorial games in the Roman Empire. The first recorded evidence of female gladiators dates back to the 1st century BCE, and they were mentioned by various ancient writers, including Juvenal and Martial.

Female gladiators were often slaves or convicted criminals who were forced to participate in the games. Some women also volunteered to participate in the games, either for financial gain or for personal reasons. Gladiatrices would fight each other or exotic animals, and in some cases, they would even be paired against male gladiators.

The use of female gladiators was not without controversy in ancient Rome. Some members of Roman society saw their participation in the games as a violation of traditional gender norms, and there was opposition to their use. In AD 200, the emperor Septimius Severus banned the participation of women in gladiatorial games, and the tradition of female gladiators slowly faded into obscurity.

However, despite the ban, evidence of female gladiators has been found in various parts of the Roman Empire, including Britain and Egypt. Inscriptions, tombstones, and other artifacts provide evidence of their existence and offer a glimpse into their lives and the role they played in the games.

In conclusion, while female gladiators were not a common sight in ancient Rome, they were an important part of the history of gladiatorial games in the Roman Empire. They offer a fascinating glimpse into the lives of women in the ancient world and the role they played in the brutal world of the arena.

THE WORLDS MOST SUCCESSFUL PIRATE WAS A PROSTITUTE FROM CHINA

1810

Ching Shih, also known as Zheng Shi, was a Chinese pirate who operated in the South China Sea during the early 19th century. She was born in 1775 and lived in Canton (now Guangzhou) where she worked as a prostitute. She married a pirate named Cheng I and after his death, she took over his fleet and became one of the most successful pirate leaders in history.

Ching Shih commanded a fleet of hundreds of ships and thousands of pirates and was known for her strict code of conduct. Her rules, known as the "Ching Code," were strictly enforced and any pirate who broke them faced severe punishment, including death. Despite her reputation for cruelty, she was also known for her sense of fairness and justice, and many sailors joined her fleet because they felt they would be treated better under her command than by other pirate captains.

Ching Shih's success was due in part to her strategic alliances with other pirate fleets and her willingness to negotiate with the Chinese and Portuguese authorities. She also had a formidable naval force, with heavily armed ships and expert navigators, and was known to be a fearless fighter.

Her pirate reign came to an end in 1810 when the Chinese government offered her amnesty in exchange for her surrender. She accepted the offer and retired from piracy, opening a gambling house in Canton. She died in 1844 at the age of 69.

Despite her infamous reputation, Ching Shih remains a legendary figure in Chinese history and is remembered as one of the world's most successful pirate captains.

THE REAL 'AVENGERS' WERE NAZI HUNTERS DURING WW2

1939-1945

During World War II, a group of real-life heroes, known as the "Avengers," worked to protect freedom and defeat the Axis powers. Unlike their fictional Marvel Comics counterpart, the real-life Avengers were comprised of military personnel, spies, and resistance fighters from various countries.

One of the most prominent members of this group was British secret agent Vera Atkins. She worked for the Special Operations Executive (SOE) and was responsible for recruiting and training female agents who were sent behind enemy lines in Nazi-occupied France to work with the French resistance.

Another key player in the real-life Avengers was U.S. Army Captain William J. Donovan, who headed the Office of Strategic Services (OSS), the predecessor of the CIA. He played a crucial role in coordinating intelligence and special operations during the war and was known for his bravery and resourcefulness.

These real-life Avengers also included members of the French resistance, Soviet spies, and Allied soldiers who served in various capacities. However, some of their methods were controversial, including the use of poison to kill prisoners of war (POWs). This controversial tactic was considered a necessary evil by some in order to gain a strategic advantage and protect their own forces.

While the real-life Avengers of World War II may not have had superpowers or high-tech gadgets, they were still heroes in their own right. Their bravery, selflessness, and willingness to do whatever was necessary to defeat the enemy helped pave the way for an Allied victory in the war.

THE OLYMPICS USED TO HOST ART COMPETITIONS

1912-1948

The Olympic Art Competitions, held as part of the Summer Olympics from 1912 to 1948, were a unique aspect of the Games that showcased the relationship between sport and art. The competitions included events in architecture, literature, music, painting, and sculpture and were open to artists of all nationalities. The winning entries were awarded medals, with gold, silver, and bronze given to the top three artists in each category.

The first Olympic Art Competitions were held at the 1912 Summer Olympics in Stockholm and were held at every Summer Olympics until 1948, except for the 1916, 1940, and 1944 Games, which were cancelled due to World War I and World War II. The artworks were judged by a panel of experts in each respective field, and the winning entries were displayed at the Games, helping to promote the arts and establish their importance as a part of the Olympic movement.

Despite their popularity and impact, the Olympic Art Competitions were dropped from the Summer Olympics after 1948 and have not been held since. Today, they remain a little-known but significant chapter in the history of the Olympic Games, highlighting the close relationship between sport and art and showcasing the important role that the arts have played in the Olympic movement.

The Olympic Art Competitions represented a unique opportunity for artists to showcase their work on a global stage and to participate in the Olympic movement. They helped to promote cross-cultural exchange and bring attention to the importance of the arts in society, making them an important part of the Olympic legacy.

KETCHUP WAS INITIALLY SOLD AS MEDICINE

1830

Ketchup was indeed sold as a type of medicine in the 1830s, during a time when the concept of a processed condiment was relatively new. The origins of ketchup can be traced back to ancient China, where it was made from fermented fish, but the modern version of ketchup as we know it today did not exist until the late 1700s.

In the early 1800s, ketchup was considered a type of condiment that was used to enhance the flavor of food. However, some enterprising individuals saw an opportunity to market ketchup as a medicine, given its reputation as a food that was believed to have health benefits.

In the 1830s, ketchup was sold as a cure-all tonic, marketed as a treatment for various ailments such as indigestion, jaundice, and scurvy. Bottles of ketchup were labeled with claims such as "A Powerful Tonic for the Blood" and "A Sure Cure for All Disorders of the Stomach". Some advertisements even claimed that ketchup had the power to ward off disease and improve overall health.

It's worth noting that, during this time, the composition of ketchup was very different from what it is today. Ketchup in the 1830s was typically made from a mixture of spices, herbs, and vegetables, and it was often sold in a liquid form. It was not until later in the 19th century that the modern, tomato-based version of ketchup became popular.

In any case, the marketing of ketchup as a medicine in the 1830s was a clever tactic that helped to establish ketchup as a popular and valuable product. While it may seem strange today, the sale of ketchup as a type of medicine in the 1830s was a testament to the versatility and adaptability of this popular condiment.

PRESIDENT ABRAHAM LINCOLN IS IN THE WRESLTING HALL OF FAME

1992

Abraham Lincoln, the 16th President of the United States, was indeed a wrestler and was inducted into the National Wrestling Hall of Fame in 1992. He was known to be a skilled wrestler in his youth and was recorded to have won approximately 300 matches out of approximately 400 contests during his lifetime.

Lincoln's wrestling career took place before he became president and was largely unknown to the general public until many years after his death. However, in the late 19th and early 20th centuries, as wrestling became more organized and regulated, Lincoln's reputation as a wrestler began to emerge.

In the early 20th century, wrestling historian William Muldoon wrote about Lincoln's wrestling career and helped to establish him as a notable figure in the history of wrestling. Muldoon described Lincoln as a "cool, determined, and powerful wrestler" and emphasized the role that wrestling played in shaping Lincoln's character and helping him to develop his physical and mental toughness.

In 1992, Lincoln was officially inducted into the National Wrestling Hall of Fame, which is dedicated to recognizing and preserving the legacy of wrestling in the United States. He was inducted as an Outstanding American, which recognizes individuals who have made significant contributions to the sport of wrestling, but who have not necessarily competed as wrestlers.

Abraham Lincoln was indeed a wrestler and is now recognized for his achievements in the sport by the National Wrestling Hall of Fame. His induction serves as a testament to his athletic prowess and helps to shed light on an often-overlooked aspect of his life and legacy.

PRESIDENT GEORGE WASHINGTONOPENED A SUCCESSFUL WHISKEY DISTILLERY

1771

Yes, it's true that after his presidency, George Washington opened a successful whiskey distillery at his Mount Vernon estate. The distillery was one of the largest and most technologically advanced of its time, and it produced a variety of spirits, including whiskey.

Washington was a well-known lover of whiskey, and he was said to have enjoyed the drink both for its taste and for its potential as a profitable business venture. He first became interested in distillation in the 1760s and built his first still in 1771. However, it was after his presidency, in 1797, that he decided to build a commercial-scale distillery at Mount Vernon.

Washington's distillery was designed and built with the help of Scottish-born distiller James Anderson, who was one of the leading experts in the field at the time. The distillery was equipped with the latest technology, including a large copper still, a malt house, and a gristmill. It was capable of producing 11,000 gallons of whiskey per year and quickly became one of the largest whiskey producers in the country.

Washington was actively involved in the management of the distillery and took great pride in its success. He kept detailed records of the production and sales of the whiskey and worked closely with Anderson to ensure that the quality of the product was of the highest standard.

After Washington's death in 1799, the distillery continued to operate under the management of his estate, and it remained a successful business venture for many years. Today, a reconstruction of the original distillery can be found at Mount Vernon, and it serves as a testament to Washington's entrepreneurial spirit and his love of whiskey.

PRESIDENT ANDREW JACKSON'S CURSING PARROT

1829-1837

Andrew Jackson, the 7th President of the United States, owned a pet parrot named Polly. The story of Jackson's parrot and its ability to curse like a sailor is a well-known anecdote from Jackson's presidency, and it has become an enduring part of his legacy.

According to accounts, Polly was a gift to Jackson and was a popular member of the household at the White House. She was known for her colorful language and was said to have learned to swear and use vulgar language from her former owner, a sailor.

Polly was a fixture at the White House and was said to be present at many important events and meetings. She was reportedly a favorite of Jackson's, and he was said to have enjoyed her company and her ability to entertain guests with her foul language.

However, Polly's language was also a source of controversy, and her presence at the White House was said to have caused offense to some visitors and members of the public. Despite this, Jackson was said to have been fond of Polly and to have considered her a valued member of his household.

In conclusion, Andrew Jackson did indeed own a pet parrot named Polly, and the story of her ability to curse like a sailor is a well-known and enduring part of his legacy. Whether or not the parrot actually swore or used vulgar language is a matter of some debate, but the story of Jackson and his foul-mouthed pet has become an enduring part of American folklore.

ALL ANCIENT OLYMPIC ATHLETES COMPETED FULLY NAKED

776 BCE - 4 AD

In the ancient Olympic Games, which were held in Olympia, Greece, athletes competed in the nude. This practice was seen as a symbol of the athletes' physical prowess and athletic ability, and it was believed that competing naked would allow spectators to see their bodies and admire their athletic form.

The ancient Olympic Games were held in honor of Zeus and were one of the most important religious and athletic events of the ancient world. They were held every four years and attracted athletes from all over Greece, who came to compete in a variety of events, including running, jumping, wrestling, and chariot racing.

The ancient Greeks placed great importance on the human form, and the ideal athletic body was seen as a symbol of physical strength and beauty. By competing naked, the athletes were able to showcase their athletic ability and to demonstrate their physical prowess to the spectators.

In conclusion, it's true that in the ancient Olympic Games, athletes competed in the nude. This practice was seen as a symbol of the athletes' physical prowess and athletic ability, and it was believed that competing naked would allow spectators to admire their athletic form. The ancient Olympic Games were an important event in ancient Greece and were held in honor of Zeus, attracting athletes from all over the country to compete in a variety of athletic events.

PEOPLE MADE CLOTHES OUT OF FOOD BAGS DURING THE GREAT DEPRESSION

1929

During the Great Depression, which lasted from 1929 to the late 1930s, many people were struggling with financial hardship and poverty. This period was characterized by high unemployment, widespread poverty, and a shortage of resources. In response to these challenges, people were forced to be resourceful and make do with what they had. One common practice was the use of food sacks, made from sturdy cotton or burlap, as a material for clothing and other household items.

Food sacks were widely available and often printed with the logos of the companies that produced the food, such as flour or sugar. They could be easily cut and sewn into a variety of clothing items, including dresses, pants, and shirts. The bags could also be dyed or painted to change their appearance, and they were often used to make household items, such as curtains, rugs, and even bedspreads.

The use of food sacks as a material for clothing and other items was not just a matter of necessity, but also a way of stretching budgets and being creative. People were able to make functional and durable clothing and household items from a readily available and affordable material, allowing them to make the most of what they had.

In conclusion, the Great Depression was a period of widespread financial hardship and poverty, but it was also a time when people were forced to be resourceful and creative. The use of food sacks as a material for clothing and other household items was one way that people were able to make the most of what they had and stretch their limited budgets. This practice remains a testament to the ingenuity and resilience of people during a challenging period in history.

PEOPLE USED TO DRESS UP DEAD RELATIVES FOR PHOTOGRAPHS

1837 - 1901

The practice of taking post-mortem photographs, also known as memorial or mourning photographs, was widespread during the Victorian era, which lasted from 1837 to 1901. This was a time of significant cultural and technological change, and several factors contributed to the popularity of post-mortem photography.

Photography was a relatively new and rapidly advancing technology during the Victorian era, and it was becoming more accessible and affordable to the general public. This made it possible for people to preserve memories of loved ones through photographs. The Victorian era was also marked by a strong emphasis on death and mourning, and many people believed that capturing a final image of their loved ones was an important part of the grieving process.

Post-mortem photographs were usually taken in the home or in a studio and were typically posed in a lifelike manner, either sitting or lying down, and dressed in their best clothing. The photographs were often displayed in the home as a reminder of the deceased and were sometimes included in funeral announcements or kept as mementos to be shared with friends and family.

In addition to these cultural factors, advancements in photography technology also played a role in the popularity of post-mortem photography. Photographers developed new techniques to make post-mortem photographs look more lifelike, such as using glass eyes or using a thin piece of fabric to drape over the face to conceal signs of decay. This made it possible to create images that were visually appealing and respectful, even after death.

The practice of taking post-mortem photographs was widespread during the Victorian era, and several cultural and technological factors contributed to its popularity. These photographs provide a fascinating glimpse into the Victorian culture of death and mourning and remain an interesting and evocative part of the cultural heritage of this era.

THE SHORTEST WAR IN HISTORY LASTED ONLY 38 MINUTES

August 27, 1896

The Anglo-Zanzibar War, which took place on 27 August 1896, is widely considered to be the shortest war in recorded history. The conflict was fought between the United Kingdom and the Zanzibar Sultanate, a small island state off the coast of East Africa that was a British protectorate.

The cause of the war was the death of Sultan Hamad bin Thuwaini on 25 August 1896, and the subsequent succession of Sultan Khalid bin Barghash. The British had preferred another candidate, Hamoud bin Mohammed, to succeed to the throne, and they demanded that Khalid step down. When Khalid refused, the British issued an ultimatum, which was rejected. In response, the British mounted a naval bombardment of the capital city of Zanzibar, which lasted 38 minutes.

During the bombardment, Khalid sought refuge in the German consulate, but he was later arrested by the British and exiled to Seychelles. The bombardment resulted in the deaths of around 500 people and the destruction of much of the city's infrastructure. After the war, the British installed their preferred candidate, Hamoud, as the new Sultan of Zanzibar.

In conclusion, the Anglo-Zanzibar War lasted just 38 minutes and remains one of the shortest conflicts in recorded history. The war marked the beginning of increased British control over East Africa and had far-reaching consequences for the region and its people.

TUG OF WAR USED TO BE THE MOST POPULAR OLYMPIC SPORT

1896 - 1920

Tug of War was once considered a sport and was included as an Olympic event in the early modern Olympic Games, which were held from 1896 to 1920. It was considered a demonstration sport at the 1904 Summer Olympics in St. Louis, Missouri, and was later added as a full medal event in the 1908 Summer Olympics in London, England.

Tug of War was played by two teams of eight athletes each, who pulled on opposite ends of a rope in an attempt to pull their opponents across a center line. The rules of the sport were similar to those used in modern-day tug of war competitions, with the winning team being the one that successfully pulled their opponents across the center line, or the team that held the rope motionless for the longest time.

The sport was popular in many countries and was seen as a test of strength and teamwork. However, by the mid-1920s, tug of war was removed from the Olympic program due to concerns over the physical strain it placed on athletes and the potential for injury.

In conclusion, tug of war was once an Olympic sport, but it was eventually removed from the Olympic program due to concerns over its physical demands and the potential for injury. Despite this, tug of war remains a popular sport in many countries, and continues to be played in regional and national competitions around the world.

OXORD UNIVERSITY IS OLDER THAN THE GREAT AZTEZ EMPIRE

1096

The University of Oxford, located in Oxford, England, is widely regarded as one of the oldest and most prestigious universities in the world. Its foundation can be traced back to the 11th century, with evidence suggesting it was established sometime between 1096 and 1167. This makes the University of Oxford older than the Aztec Empire, which was a powerful Mesoamerican civilization that emerged in the 14th century and reached its peak in the 15th and 16th centuries.

Oxford has a long and rich history, and has been a center of learning and intellectual advancement for over 900 years. Over the centuries, the university has produced numerous Nobel Prize winners, Fields Medal recipients, and other notable figures in fields such as science, literature, and politics. The university has also been instrumental in shaping the cultural and intellectual landscape of the modern world, and has been home to many of the world's most brilliant minds.

The Aztec Empire, on the other hand, was a complex and highly organized civilization that was located in what is now Mexico. It is well known for its sophisticated culture, impressive architecture, and advanced agricultural systems, as well as its remarkable religious practices and rich mythology. The Aztecs left a lasting impact on the world and are widely considered to have been one of the most influential civilizations in the pre-Columbian Americas.

In conclusion, while the Aztec Empire was a remarkable civilization with a rich cultural heritage, the University of Oxford predates it by several centuries and continues to be one of the oldest and most prestigious universities in the world. Its long and storied history, combined with its ongoing commitment to intellectual and cultural advancement, make Oxford a unique and important institution in the world of higher education.

THE MOST HISTORICALLY POPULAR SERIAL KILLER

16TH CENTURY

Elizabeth Báthory, also known as the "Blood Countess," was a notorious female serial killer from Hungary who lived in the late 16th and early 17th centuries. She was born into a wealthy and powerful noble family and was considered one of the richest women in Hungary during her time. Despite her privileged upbringing, she developed a reputation for sadism and cruelty, especially towards the young servant girls who worked in her castle.

It is estimated that Elizabeth Báthory committed hundreds of murders, with some reports suggesting that she may have killed as many as 650 girls and young women. Her methods of torture and murder were brutal, including beating, burning, and even starvation. Her crimes were only discovered after one of the survivors escaped and alerted the authorities.

Elizabeth Báthory was eventually arrested and sentenced to life imprisonment in her own castle, where she died several years later. The exact number of her victims remains unknown, and the motivations behind her crimes continue to be the subject of much speculation.

Over the years, Elizabeth Báthory has become one of the most infamous female serial killers in history, and her story has been retold and sensationalized in various books, films, and plays. Despite the passage of time, her legacy continues to fascinate and horrify people to this day, and she remains one of the most notorious figures in the annals of crime and punishment.

FIRST MEDALS OF HONOR AWARDED IN THE CIVIL WAR

March 25, 1863

The Medal of Honor, the highest military decoration that can be awarded by the United States government, was established on July 12, 1862, as a way to recognize acts of valor and bravery by Union soldiers during the Civil War.

The first Medals of Honor were awarded on March 25, 1863, to six Union soldiers for their actions at the Battle of New Bern, North Carolina. These six soldiers demonstrated exceptional courage and bravery in the face of enemy fire, setting the standard for what it means to be awarded the Medal of Honor.

Since its inception, the criteria for the Medal of Honor have evolved over time to reflect changing circumstances and the evolving nature of warfare. As a result, the medal has been awarded to members of various branches of the military, including the Army, Navy, and Air Force, for acts of heroism and bravery in a variety of conflicts, including the Spanish-American War, World War I, World War II, the Korean War, the Vietnam War, and more recent conflicts in Iraq and Afghanistan.

The Medal of Honor is widely regarded as one of the highest honors that can be bestowed upon an American service member, and it continues to symbolize the bravery and selflessness of those who serve in the military. To this day, the medal remains one of the most prestigious awards in the world, and it serves as a testament to the courage and bravery of the men and women who have served their country in the military.

PINEAPPLES WERE ONCE CONSIDERED A STATUS SYMBOL

18th CENTURY

The use of pineapples as a symbol of wealth and prestige in 18th century England was a reflection of the fruit's rarity and exclusivity. Pineapples were imported from the West Indies, which was seen as a desirable and exotic destination, and their transportation and preservation was costly, making them a luxury item only accessible to the wealthy.

The obsession with pineapples as a symbol of status was evident in various forms of art and architecture. Pineapple motifs and carvings became a popular aspect of interior design and the fruit was frequently depicted in paintings and sculptures. Additionally, many homes and gardens incorporated pineapples into their design as a symbol of wealth and luxury, with some even featuring structures shaped like pineapples.

The display of pineapples in prominent locations, such as at the front gate or entrance hall of a home, became a common way to show off one's wealth and hospitality. The fruit was also frequently used as a centerpiece at formal gatherings and banquets, further emphasizing its association with high society.

In conclusion, the use of pineapples as a status symbol in 18th century England was a result of the fruit's rarity, cost, and association with the exotic West Indies. Its popularity and incorporation into various forms of art and architecture further solidified its position as a symbol of wealth and luxury.

THE ANCIENT GREEK BELIEVED REDHEADED PEOPLE BECAME VAMPIRES AFTER DEATH

400 BCE

The belief that redheads turned into vampires after death was a prevalent superstition in ancient Greek society, dating back to the mythology and folklore of the era. This belief was rooted in the stereotype that redheads were known for their fiery and unpredictable personalities.

According to Greek myth, red hair was seen as a sign of a strong connection to the underworld, making redheads more susceptible to becoming vampires after death. These individuals were feared for their potentially vengeful spirits, which could continue to wreak havoc on the living even after death.

As a result of these beliefs, redheads were often shunned or avoided by some communities, who sought to ward off their perceived vampiric tendencies through various rituals and talismans.

It's important to note that this belief about redheads and vampirism was specific to ancient Greek culture and may not have been widely held in other civilizations. However, it serves as an interesting example of how physical traits could be linked to supernatural beliefs and how these beliefs could shape how individuals were perceived and treated.

KNOCKER-UPPERS WERE HUMAN ALARM CLOCKS

19TH-20TH CENTURY

In the late 19th and early 20th centuries, many people in the UK lived in areas where it was difficult to hear the sound of an alarm clock. To solve this problem, people known as "knocker-uppers" were hired to physically go to the homes of people who needed to be woken up for work and knock on their windows. The knocker-uppers would carry a long pole with a soft end, which they would use to tap on the windows of their clients.

This profession was most common in the industrial cities of England, where factory workers had to be up at the crack of dawn to start their shifts. The knocker-uppers would typically work in the early hours of the morning and would have a large round of clients to visit. They would use their own discretion to judge the best time to wake each person, taking into account factors such as their work schedule and whether they had gone to bed late the night before.

The profession of knocker-upper became less necessary as the use of alarm clocks became more widespread, and eventually disappeared altogether. However, it serves as a reminder of the ingenuity and resourcefulness of people in the past who found ways to solve everyday problems, even when technology was not as advanced as it is today.

THE EXPLOSION THAT SPARKED THE SPANISH-AMERICAN WAR

February 15, 1898

The explosion of the USS Maine in Havana Harbor on February 15, 1898 was a seminal event in American history that led to the country's entry into the Spanish-American War. The USS Maine was a second-class battleship that was sent to Havana to protect American interests in the region. On the night of February 15, a massive explosion rocked the ship, causing extensive damage and killing 266 crew members.

At the time, there was much speculation about the cause of the explosion, with many people blaming the Spanish. This speculation was fueled by anti-Spanish sentiment in the United States and the political tensions between the two countries. The United States declared war on Spain just a few months later, and the Spanish-American War began.

However, subsequent investigations into the incident revealed that the explosion was most likely caused by a naval mine, rather than an attack by the Spanish. The exact circumstances surrounding the placement of the mine remain unclear to this day, with some theories suggesting that it was placed there by pro-independence Cuban militants.

Regardless of the cause, the explosion of the USS Maine was a significant event that had far-reaching consequences. It was widely covered by the press and became a rallying cry for war, with many newspapers using headlines such as "Remember the Maine, to Hell with Spain!" The event was also a turning point in American foreign policy, marking the country's first foray into international conflict as a world power.

Today, the USS Maine is remembered as a symbol of American bravery and sacrifice, and the events surrounding its explosion continue to be studied by historians and enthusiasts alike. The incident remains a fascinating and intriguing chapter in American history, one that continues to be remembered and discussed over a century later.

A DANGEROUS PLAN TO ESCAPE AUTHORITARIAN GERMANY

September, 1979

The story of two families who attempted to escape from East Germany in the 1970s is a tale of bravery, determination, and risk-taking. East Germany was a communist state that was part of the Soviet bloc, and it was known for its strict surveillance and control over its citizens. In the 1970s, many people living in East Germany sought to escape the country due to political repression and economic hardship.

Two families came up with a daring plan to escape to the West. They would build a hot air balloon and fly over the heavily guarded border that separated East and West Germany. The plan was ambitious and dangerous, as the East German government had a shoot-to-kill policy for anyone attempting to cross the border.

Despite the risks, the families spent months secretly building the hot air balloon in a barn on the outskirts of the city. They collected materials, tested the balloon, and trained for the flight. Finally, the day came when they felt they were ready to make the attempt.

The families set off in the dead of night, flying their balloon over the border into West Germany. The flight was not without its challenges, as they encountered strong winds and had to make several adjustments to stay aloft. But eventually, they landed safely in West Germany, where they were greeted with joy and relief by friends and family.

The story of these two families is an example of the incredible bravery and determination of people who lived under oppressive regimes. Their successful escape was a testament to the human spirit and the desire for freedom. Although their story is not well-known, it is a powerful reminder of the lengths that people will go to in order to live in a free and democratic society.

A RADICAL PLAN TO CONQUER EVEREST

1933

In 1933, British World War I veteran Maurice Wilson hatched an unorthodox plan to reach the still-untouched summit of Mount Everest. Wilson was a mountaineer with limited experience, but he was driven by a strong desire to prove himself and to make a name for himself in the world of mountaineering.

Wilson's plan was to fly a small plane to a high altitude and then continue on foot to the summit of Everest. This was a radical departure from the traditional method of climbing Everest, which involved months of acclimatization and gradual ascent from base camp.

Wilson's solo attempt to reach the summit of Everest began in 1933 when he took off from England in a single-engine plane and flew to India. From there, he continued on to Darjeeling, where he began his journey on foot. Despite facing numerous obstacles and setbacks, including a crash-landing in the Himalayas and a lack of proper equipment and supplies, Wilson persevered and continued his journey.

Unfortunately, Wilson's quest to reach the summit of Everest came to an end when he was last seen alive near the mountain's base camp. It is believed that he died due to exposure or altitude sickness.

While Wilson's attempt to reach the summit of Everest was ultimately unsuccessful, his story is a testament to the human spirit and the drive to conquer the unknown. Wilson's daring attempt inspired many future mountaineers and adventurers, and his legacy continues to live on today.

A SCHEME TO BECOME THE RICHEST PERSON ON EARTH

December 4, 1924

In 1924, a Portuguese businessman named Francisco Manuel Homem Cristo, who was facing bankruptcy, launched an audacious international scheme to become one of the wealthiest men in the world. Cristo became known for his flamboyant personality and his extravagant lifestyle, which included a yacht and a collection of luxury cars.

Cristo's scheme involved a plan to take advantage of the high demand for gold during the early 1920s by selling fraudulent gold-mining concessions in Angola, which was then a Portuguese colony. He convinced wealthy investors from Portugal and other countries to invest in his gold-mining venture, promising high returns on their investment.

However, Cristo's scheme was based on false promises and fraudulent representations, and the gold mines he claimed to have been non-existent. He used the funds raised from investors to finance his lavish lifestyle, but eventually, the truth about his scheme was uncovered and he was arrested and charged with fraud.

Cristo's audacious scheme was a reminder of the importance of due diligence and caution when investing in any business venture. It also demonstrated the consequences of fraudulent behavior and the impact it can have on individuals and the wider community.

Despite his criminal past, Cristo became a controversial figure in Portuguese society, with some people seeing him as a Robin Hood-style figure who took from the rich to give to the poor, while others saw him as a criminal who took advantage of innocent people for his own personal gain. His story remains a subject of fascination and debate in Portugal to this day.

TRESPASSING ON MOUNT ST. HELENS

December 4, 1924

Robert Rogers, a man with a history of trespassing and a fascination with dangerous and restricted areas, set his sights on Mount St. Helens in the spring of 1980. Mount St. Helens was a popular tourist destination at the time, but it was also an active volcano that was known to be potentially hazardous.

Despite the warnings of park rangers and other officials, Rogers insisted on climbing the mountain, even as seismic activity and other signs indicated that an eruption was imminent. On May 18, 1980, Mount St. Helens erupted in one of the most devastating volcanic eruptions in American history. The eruption claimed the lives of 57 people, including Rogers, who was found dead near the base of the mountain.

Rogers' death was a tragedy and a reminder of the dangers of disregarding the warnings of experts and of pursuing personal goals at the expense of safety. The eruption of Mount St. Helens was a major natural disaster, and it had far-reaching impacts on the local community and the environment.

Despite the risks and dangers associated with volcanic activity, Mount St. Helens continues to attract visitors today, and it is now a popular destination for hikers and tourists. However, visitors are reminded of the potential hazards and are encouraged to follow safety guidelines and the advice of park officials.

A RUNAWAY NAZI AND A CHASE AROUND THE WORLD

May 11, 1960

The true story of the pursuit of Adolf Eichmann, a top Nazi official and one of the main architects of the Holocaust, by Israeli Mossad agent Peter Malkin is a tale of determination, bravery, and justice. After World War II, Eichmann fled to South America, where he lived under an assumed identity for nearly a decade.

In the late 1950s, the Israeli government tasked Malkin with finding and capturing Eichmann. The Mossad agent spent months gathering information and following leads, eventually tracking Eichmann down to a neighborhood in Buenos Aires, Argentina. On May 11, 1960, Malkin and a team of Mossad agents apprehended Eichmann and brought him back to Israel to stand trial for his crimes.

Eichmann's trial, which began on April 11, 1961, was one of the first and most important war crimes trials in history. He was charged with 15 counts of crimes against humanity, war crimes, and crimes against the Jewish people. The trial lasted nearly four months and included testimony from Holocaust survivors and other witnesses. On December 15, 1961, Eichmann was found guilty on all charges and sentenced to death. He was executed on June 1, 1962.

The pursuit and capture of Adolf Eichmann was a major turning point in the effort to bring Nazi war criminals to justice and to ensure that the world never forgets the atrocities committed during the Holocaust. It was a testament to the bravery of those who pursued justice and to the resilience of the Jewish people, who, even in the face of unspeakable horrors, refused to give up their fight for survival and dignity. Today, Eichmann's capture and trial continue to serve as an important reminder of the need to hold those who commit horrific crimes accountable and to continue the struggle against hate and intolerance in all its forms.

THE NEVER-ENDING LAS VEGAS FLIGHT

March 17, 1958

The true story of the 1958 "Never-ending Flight" of a modified airplane out of Las Vegas is a fascinating episode in aviation history. The flight, which was part of a publicity stunt by the Sinclair Oil Company, was intended to showcase the efficiency of Sinclair's new gasoline formula, Dino-Fuel, by setting a new world record for continuous flight.

On March 17, 1958, a modified B-29 Superfortress bomber took off from McCarran Airport in Las Vegas with a crew of five and a single objective: to stay aloft for as long as possible without landing. The plane was loaded with enough fuel, food, and supplies to keep the crew aloft for several days, and its engines were specially modified to run on Dino-Fuel, a gasoline formula that was touted by Sinclair as being significantly more efficient than other fuels of the time.

The flight quickly captured the attention of the public and the media, and people around the world tuned in to follow the progress of the never-ending flight. The flight broke several world records for continuous flight, and the crew remained aloft for over 64 days, setting a new world record that still stands to this day.

Despite the success of the flight, it was not without its challenges and dangers. The crew had to deal with engine problems, fuel leaks, and other technical issues, and they had to improvise and adapt as they encountered new challenges. The close quarters and the monotony of life in the air also took a toll on the crew, who had to work together to keep their spirits up and maintain their focus on their goal.

In the end, the never-ending flight of the B-29 Superfortress was a remarkable feat of human endurance and aviation technology. It demonstrated the efficiency of Dino-Fuel and cemented Sinclair's place in aviation history, and it remains a testament to the ingenuity and determination of the human spirit.

FROM POVERTY TO ONE OF THE MOST PROMINENT FIGURES IN CHINA

20ᵗʰ CENTURY

Du Yuesheng, also known as Big-Eared Du, was a Chinese underworld figure who rose to become one of the most influential and powerful figures in modern China. Born in the late 19th century in Shanghai, Du grew up in poverty and was drawn to the city's criminal underworld at an early age. Through a combination of cunning, intelligence, and brute force, he rose through the ranks to become one of the most feared and respected gangsters in Shanghai. Du's influence extended far beyond the criminal underworld, however. He had close ties with the Nationalist Party and was a key player in the power struggles and political maneuverings that characterized early 20th-century China. He was also a master of guanxi, the complex network of personal relationships that is so crucial to conducting business and wielding power in China. Through these connections, he built a vast network of influence that reached into the highest levels of government, commerce, and society.

Despite his fearsome reputation, Du was a complex and multifaceted figure. He was known for his intelligence and business acumen, as well as his generosity and philanthropy. He was also an early advocate of anti-Japanese sentiment and helped fund the resistance against Japan during their occupation of China in the 1930s and 1940s. Despite his importance, however, Du's role in modern Chinese history has often been overlooked and downplayed. The Communist Party, which came to power in 1949, saw him as a symbol of the corruption and decadence of the old order and sought to erase his legacy. As a result, much of his story has been lost to history.

Today, Du Yuesheng remains one of the most enigmatic and overlooked figures in modern Chinese history. He was a man of contradictions and extremes, a symbol of the chaos and violence of the early 20th century, as well as the power and influence that can be wielded by those who are savvy and cunning enough to navigate the complex landscape of Chinese society. Despite his largely forgotten legacy, his story continues to be a testament to the enduring influence of the underworld in China and to the power of the human spirit to rise from humble beginnings to great heights.

THE MAN WHO DECIEVED JEWS DURING WW2 AFTER GAINING THEIR TRUST

1943

In Nazi-occupied Paris during World War II, a man known as "Dr. Eugène" emerged as a beacon of hope for the Jewish population. He offered a way out of the city, promising to help Jews escape the clutches of the Nazi regime and the impending deportations to the death camps.

"Dr. Eugène," whose real name was Eugène Weisz, was a Hungarian-born businessman and a member of the French Resistance. He established an escape network that operated in and around Paris, helping Jews escape to safety. The network was highly organized and operated with the help of other Resistance members and sympathetic individuals.

However, "Dr. Eugène" and his network were not what they seemed. The escape routes he promised were often dangerous and treacherous, and many Jews who sought his help ended up in the hands of the Gestapo. It later emerged that "Dr. Eugène" was working for the Gestapo and that his entire escape network was a trap designed to ensnare Jews and deliver them into the hands of the Nazi regime.

Despite this, "Dr. Eugène" managed to maintain his cover for several years and continued to deceive Jews and members of the Resistance. He was eventually arrested by the Allies in 1944 and exposed as a Gestapo agent. He was later tried and sentenced to life in prison for his role in the capture and extermination of hundreds of Jews.

The story of "Dr. Eugène" is a sobering reminder of the dangers and deceit that Jews faced in Nazi-occupied France. It also serves as a tribute to the bravery and selflessness of those who risked their lives to help others escape the horrors of the Holocaust. Despite the evil deeds of people like "Dr. Eugène," the bravery and compassion of those who worked to save Jews from the Nazis will always be remembered as a shining example of the power of the human spirit to triumph over evil.

CASTAWAYS OF THE INDIAN OCEAN

July 31, 1761

The true story of castaways on a lost and hostile scrap of land that occurred on July 31, 1761 was the story of the survivors of the wreck of the French ship "St. Jean." The ship was on a voyage from France to Mauritius when it encountered a severe storm in the Indian Ocean. Despite the efforts of the crew, the ship was badly damaged and eventually ran aground on a remote and uninhabited island.

The castaways were faced with a number of challenges as they tried to survive on the island. The island was barren and lacked fresh water, food, and shelter, and the castaways were forced to improvise in order to survive. They managed to build a shelter using materials salvaged from the ship and were able to find some food and water, but their situation was far from ideal.

The castaways were also plagued by other difficulties, including conflicts with one another, and the danger posed by the island's hostile environment. The island was home to a number of dangerous animals, including snakes and large birds, and the castaways were constantly on guard in order to protect themselves.

Despite these challenges, the castaways managed to survive for several months on the island. Eventually, they were rescued by a passing ship and taken to safety. The story of their survival is a testament to the ingenuity and resourcefulness of the human spirit, and has been the subject of many books, films, and other works of art.

However, it is worth noting that the castaways' misfortune was due in part to the actions of the French crew, who had ignored warnings about the storm and sailed into danger. The story serves as a cautionary tale about the dangers of recklessness and the importance of taking precautions when traveling on the high seas.

THE DOWNFALL OF A VISIONARY
1943

Nikolai Vavilov was a Russian botanist and geneticist who dedicated his life to improving Soviet agriculture and ending famine. He was born in 1887 in St. Petersburg and began his career as a plant breeder, studying the genetics of crops and their geographical origins. In the early 1920s, Vavilov became the head of the newly created All-Union Institute of Plant Industry in Leningrad, where he began to develop a comprehensive program for improving Soviet agriculture.

Vavilov believed that the key to improving agriculture was to find and collect the world's most diverse and valuable crops, and then to use these crops to breed new, hardier, and higher-yielding varieties. He led a team of scientists on numerous expeditions around the world, collecting over 250,000 plant specimens from more than 60 countries. He believed that the world's centers of crop diversity were located in the Mediterranean, Asia, and the Americas, and he spent much of his life studying these regions.

However, Vavilov's dedication to science and truth ultimately led to his downfall. In the late 1920s and early 1930s, Trofim Lysenko, a Soviet agronomist, rose to power in the Soviet Union and gained the support of Joseph Stalin. Lysenko rejected the principles of genetics, instead promoting a theory known as "Michurinism," which claimed that acquired traits could be passed down from generation to generation. This theory was in direct opposition to the scientific understanding of genetics, which Vavilov strongly supported. As Lysenko's influence grew, he began to attack and discredit Vavilov and his work. Vavilov was arrested in 1940 and charged with plotting against the state. He was convicted and sentenced to 20 years in a labour camp, where he died of starvation in 1943.
The legacy of Nikolai Vavilov lives on today as he is considered to be one of the founding fathers of modern plant breeding and agricultural science. Despite the efforts of Lysenko and the Soviet government to discredit him, Vavilov's work has since been vindicated, and his collection of plant specimens is now considered one of the most valuable and important collections in the world.

A MASTERPIECE BORN FROM DISCONTENT

1772

In the past, when the position of a court composer was held by someone like Franz-Joseph Haydn, who served Prince Esterházy, it was even more challenging to subtly convey a message to the boss. During the summer, the Prince took his orchestra to the cottage with him, as was the custom in those days before the invention of iPods. However, as the summer went on and on, the musicians grew increasingly discontent, separated from their wives back in Eisenstadt and frustrated with the Prince's seemingly never-ending stay.

Haydn, who was known for composing symphonies quickly, took on the task of getting his message across to the Prince. He created a new work, which the Esterházy family attended. But this was no ordinary performance. During the final slow movement, the musicians one by one stood up, extinguished the candles on their music stands, and walked off the stage, until only Haydn and the concertmaster were left playing on two muted violins.

The Prince is said to have remarked upon seeing the musicians leave, "Well, if they all leave I suppose we had better leave too." The next day, everyone returned to Vienna, indicating that Haydn's hint was successful. The "Farewell" Symphony has since become a timeless classic in classical music.

THE MYSTERIOUS DISSAPEARENCE OF A PRIME MINISTER

December 17, 1967

On 17 December 1967, Harold Holt, the then Prime Minister of Australia, went for a swim at Cheviot Beach, near Portsea, Victoria. Despite being an experienced swimmer and surrounded by several friends, Holt disappeared and was presumed to have drowned.

A massive search operation was launched but no trace of Holt was found. The circumstances of his disappearance and the fact that he was the Prime Minister of Australia at the time made it one of the most mysterious and controversial incidents in Australian history. Some conspiracy theorists even suggested that Holt had faked his own death or had been kidnapped by a foreign power.

However, the official explanation was that Holt had been caught in a strong rip current and swept out to sea. Despite extensive efforts, no remains were ever found, and the Prime Minister was officially declared dead on 19 December 1967.

His death sent shockwaves through the nation and sparked a lot of speculation and conspiracy theories, but it is widely accepted that he drowned while swimming at Cheviot Beach. Harold Holt was succeeded as Prime Minister by John Gorton.

TULSA'S TRAGIC ATTEMPT TO BE A WESTERN METROPOLIS

1920s

The story of the ill-conceived boxing match in the booming oil town of Tulsa, Oklahoma, is one that showcases the city's ambitions to become a major player in the American West. In the early 20th century, Tulsa was experiencing tremendous growth and prosperity due to the oil boom, and city leaders were eager to put Tulsa on the map and establish it as a hub of industry and culture.

One of their ideas was to host a high-profile boxing match between two top fighters, which they believed would draw in a large crowd and attract nationwide attention. They spared no expense in promoting the event, hiring some of the best boxers of the time and offering a large purse to the winner.

However, the match quickly devolved into one of the most ill-conceived boxing matches of all time. The fighters were poorly matched, and the bout quickly turned into a one-sided affair, with one fighter dominating the other. The crowd became restless, and the atmosphere turned ugly, with spectators booing and jeering the fighters.

To make matters worse, the bout ended in a controversial decision, with the judges awarding the victory to the wrong fighter. The crowd erupted in anger, and the situation soon devolved into a full-scale riot, with people throwing chairs and other objects into the ring. The police were called in to restore order, but it took several hours to calm the crowd and clear the venue.

The aftermath of the ill-fated boxing match was a major embarrassment for the city of Tulsa, and it left a lasting impression on those who witnessed it. Despite their efforts to become a western metropolis, the city's ambitions were dashed by the events of that fateful night. The ill-conceived boxing match remains a cautionary tale for those who believe that hosting high-profile sporting events is a surefire way to put a city on the map.

RELIGIOUS PERSECUTION REACHES THE BORDER

April 1, 1929

The Cristero War, also known as the Cristiada, was a religious conflict that took place in Mexico from 1926 to 1929. It was a response to the Mexican government's anti-clerical laws, which limited the power of the Roman Catholic Church and led to widespread persecution of priests and laypeople. The conflict was particularly intense in central and western Mexico, but its effects were felt across the country, including in Naco, Arizona, which was located just over the border from Mexico.

In April 1929, the violence of the Cristero War reached a fever pitch. On April 1, Mexican federal forces attacked the town of Naco, Sonora, just across the border from Naco, Arizona. The fighting was intense and lasted for several days, with both sides using heavy weaponry, including machine guns and artillery. Many residents of Naco, Arizona fled across the border to seek refuge, while others huddled in their homes, hoping to avoid the violence.

The conflict in Naco had a profound impact on the local community. Many of the residents of Naco, Arizona were Mexican-American, and they had close ties to their relatives and friends across the border. The violence and bloodshed in Naco, Sonora were a painful reminder of the dangers of the Cristero War, and many residents of Naco, Arizona were deeply disturbed by what was happening just a few miles away.

Despite the violence, the Cristero War eventually came to an end in 1929, after the Mexican government and the Catholic Church reached a compromise. The agreement allowed the Church to resume many of its previous activities, and the persecution of Catholics in Mexico came to a close. The conflict left deep scars, however, and its legacy continues to be felt in Mexico to this day. The Cristero War remains an important chapter in Mexico's history and a reminder of the power of religion and the lengths to which people will go to defend their beliefs.

BRITAIN'S MOST FAMOUS SPY

1943

Noor Inayat Khan, also known as Nora Baker, was a British spy of Indian descent who served in the Special Operations Executive (SOE) during World War II. She was born in Moscow in 1914 to an Indian father and American mother, and grew up in France.

Khan trained as a wireless operator and was sent to Nazi-occupied France in June 1943 as a secret agent for the SOE. Her task was to transmit messages between London and the French Resistance, a dangerous and difficult mission that required great bravery and skill. Despite the high risk involved, Khan continued to carry out her duties even after most of the other SOE agents in France had been captured or killed.

In October 1943, Khan was betrayed and arrested by the Gestapo. Despite being subjected to brutal interrogation and torture, she refused to reveal any information about the Resistance or her fellow agents. She was eventually transferred to the Dachau concentration camp, where she was executed in September 1944.

For her courage and selflessness, Noor Inayat Khan was posthumously awarded the Croix de Guerre and the George Cross, Britain's highest civilian award for bravery. Today, she is remembered as a hero and a symbol of resistance against fascism and oppression.

THE TRAGIC TALE OF A MATHEMATICAL PRODIGY

May 1832

Évariste Galois was a French mathematician born in 1811. He is known for his contributions to abstract algebra, particularly the theory of groups, which he developed in the early 1830s. Galois' work on groups has been described as some of the most important in the history of mathematics and has been widely studied and applied in various fields, including physics and computer science.

Aside from his mathematical achievements, Galois was also known for his political activism. He was a member of a revolutionary group that sought to overthrow the government of King Louis-Philippe. In May 1832, he was arrested and imprisoned for his political activities. While in prison, he wrote many of his mathematical papers and letters, including his famous last letter to his friend Auguste Chevalier, in which he discussed his theories on groups.

Galois was eventually released from prison, but his political activities continued to get him in trouble with the authorities. In June 1832, he was involved in a fatal duel, which was fought over a political dispute. Galois was wounded in the duel and died the next day at the age of 20.

Despite his short life, Évariste Galois left a lasting legacy in mathematics and his contributions to the field have been widely recognized and celebrated. He is considered one of the greatest mathematicians of the 19th century and his work continues to inspire new discoveries and advances in mathematics and science.

POLAND'S MOST BELOVED VETERAN WAS A GRIZZLY BEAR

1942

Wojtek was indeed a real bear who became a beloved and honored veteran of World War II. Wojtek was born in Iran in 1942 and was adopted by a group of Polish soldiers who were stationed in the region during the war. The soldiers took the bear in and raised him as one of their own, teaching him how to behave like a human and even giving him a rank in the army.

Wojtek was trained to carry ammunition for the soldiers and quickly became a valuable member of the unit, known for his strength and bravery. He even learned to salute on command and was a source of comfort and companionship for the soldiers.

Wojtek and the soldiers eventually made their way to Europe, where they fought in several battles, including the Battle of Monte Cassino in Italy. After the war, Wojtek was taken to a military transit camp in Scotland, where he became a popular attraction and was even featured in British newspapers.

In 1963, Wojtek was eventually taken to the Edinburgh Zoo, where he lived out the rest of his life. He died in 1963 and was remembered as a symbol of the close bond between soldiers and their animal companions.

Wojtek's story has become a legend in Poland, where he is remembered as a true war hero and an important part of the country's history. A statue of Wojtek now stands in Krakow, Poland, as a testament to his bravery and the special bond he shared with the soldiers who adopted him.

THE ORIGINS OF PONZI SCHEMES FROM CHARLES PONZI

1920

Charles Ponzi was an Italian-American con artist and swindler who became infamous for his eponymous Ponzi scheme. He was born in Italy in 1882 and immigrated to the United States in 1903.

Ponzi began his criminal career as a hustler, working various scams before hitting upon the idea for his Ponzi scheme in 1919. The scheme promised to deliver exceptionally high returns to investors in a short period of time, with the returns supposedly generated by buying and selling international reply coupons. In reality, however, Ponzi was using the investments of new investors to pay returns to earlier investors, creating the illusion of a profitable business.

The scheme rapidly attracted a large number of investors, many of whom were lured in by the high returns and the promise of quick riches. Ponzi became a wealthy man overnight, buying a mansion and a fleet of luxury cars, and living a lavish lifestyle. However, the scheme eventually began to unravel as the number of investors grew and the amount of money Ponzi owed skyrocketed. In 1920, the Boston Post newspaper published an investigation exposing the true nature of Ponzi's business and the fact that it was nothing more than a pyramid scheme. The news of the investigation caused a panic among investors, who rushed to withdraw their money. Ponzi tried to calm the situation by assuring investors that their funds were safe and that he would repay their investments, but it was too late. The scheme collapsed, and Ponzi was unable to repay the millions of dollars he owed to investors.

Ponzi was eventually arrested and charged with 86 counts of mail fraud. He was found guilty and sentenced to prison, where he served several years before being deported back to Italy. He died in Rio de Janeiro, Brazil in 1949, penniless and largely forgotten.

The legacy of Charles Ponzi and his scheme lives on, however, as the term "Ponzi scheme" is still used today to describe any investment scam that promises high returns with little or no risk.

THE INSPIRING STORY OF CHEETAH RACING

1950s

Kenneth Gandar-Dower was a Kenyan wildlife conservationist and animal trainer who lived in the mid-20th century. He was passionate about cheetahs and dedicated his life to protecting and conserving these magnificent animals. However, his most significant contribution to the cheetah world was his secret runaway success in training them for racing.

In the late 1950s, Gandar-Dower noticed that cheetahs were hunted and captured for their fur and were facing extinction. He decided to do something about it and started to work on a project to train cheetahs to race. He believed that by showcasing their speed and agility, he could generate interest and support for their conservation. He started with a few cheetah cubs that he rescued from hunters and began to train them using positive reinforcement techniques. Initially, he faced several challenges, including getting the cheetahs to trust him and developing a training program that would suit their unique physical and mental needs. However, he was determined and refused to give up.

After months of hard work and dedication, Gandar-Dower finally succeeded in training his cheetahs to run at incredible speeds. He then organized secret races in remote locations, inviting only a select few people to witness the remarkable feat. The races were a huge success, and the word quickly spread, generating widespread interest in cheetah racing. As more people became interested in cheetah racing, Gandar-Dower's secret project gained more recognition and popularity. He continued to train and race cheetahs, generating significant funding for cheetah conservation efforts. His innovative idea not only helped save the species from extinction but also brought attention to the importance of wildlife conservation. Gandar-Dower's secret runaway success with racing cheetahs has since inspired numerous other conservationists and animal trainers. His legacy continues to live on, and cheetah racing remains a popular sport, with races being held all over the world. His story is a testament to the power of determination and the impact that one person can have on the world.

THE FORGOTTEN VISIONARY: QUIRINO CRISTIANI

1917

Quirino Cristiani was a visionary Argentine filmmaker who made a significant impact on the world of animation during the early 20th century. Born in Buenos Aires in 1896, Cristiani showed a talent for drawing and storytelling from a young age. He went on to study art and design, eventually discovering the medium of animation and becoming fascinated by its potential to bring his stories to life.

In 1917, Cristiani made his directorial debut with the short animated film "El Apóstol". This film was groundbreaking, as it was the first full-length animated feature to be produced in the world. The film was a huge success and cemented Cristiani's reputation as a talented and innovative filmmaker. He went on to make several more animated features, including "Sincopa" and "El Negoción", which were well received by audiences and critics alike.

Cristiani's animation style was distinct and ahead of its time. He utilized innovative techniques, such as multiplane cameras and cel animation, to create dynamic and engaging stories. He also tackled complex social and political issues in his films, which made him a respected and influential figure in Argentine cinema.

Unfortunately, despite his immense talent and impact on the world of animation, Cristiani's legacy has been largely forgotten over the years. This is largely due to the fact that many of his films were destroyed in a fire at the studios where they were stored, and as a result, very few of his works survive today. Additionally, the onset of the Great Depression in the 1930s led to a decline in the demand for animated films, and Cristiani was forced to stop making movies.

Despite this, Quirino Cristiani remains an important figure in the history of animation, and his contribution to the medium should not be overlooked. He was a true pioneer and visionary, who pushed the boundaries of what was possible in animation and paved the way for future generations of filmmakers. Today, his legacy lives on, inspiring animators and filmmakers around the world to continue pushing the limits of their craft.

BREAKING THE CYCLE OF GUINEA WORM DISEASE

1981

In 1981, an outbreak of a mysterious paralytic illness occurred in northern Mozambique. This outbreak sparked the attention of the international medical community, as people started to become paralyzed for no apparent reason.

An international team of doctors was assembled to investigate the outbreak and determine the cause of the paralysis. Through careful examination of patients and review of medical records, the team was able to identify the underlying disease as Guinea worm disease (GWD), also known as dracunculiasis.

GWD is a parasitic infection caused by the larvae of the Dracunculus medinensis worm. People become infected by drinking contaminated water and the larvae burrow into the body and mature into adult worms. The adult worms eventually make their way to the surface, causing painful blisters and sores. When the blisters break, the worm emerges, leading to further contamination of the water supply.

The international team of doctors quickly sprang into action, launching a campaign to educate communities about the disease and how to prevent it. They also provided treatment for infected individuals and worked to improve access to clean water sources.

Thanks to the efforts of the international community, GWD has been significantly reduced since its identification in 1981. The World Health Organization (WHO) reports that the number of annual cases has dropped from an estimated 3.5 million in 1986 to just over 1,000 in 2021.

The true story of the 1981 outbreak of Guinea worm disease in northern Mozambique highlights the importance of international cooperation in the fight against infectious diseases and the power of medical science to save lives.

THE BRAVE WARRIOR WITH A METAL LIMB

1480

Götz von Berlichingen was a German nobleman and mercenary who lived in the late 15th and early 16th centuries. He is perhaps best known for his notoriety as a bold and daring warrior, as well as for the metal hand he had fitted after losing his right arm in battle.

Berlichingen was born in 1480 in the region of Swabia, in what is now southwestern Germany. He was raised as a member of the nobility and received a good education, but he chose to pursue a career as a mercenary rather than taking up a life of privilege and leisure. He soon gained a reputation as a brave and cunning warrior, and was much sought after by various factions and armies throughout Germany.

In 1504, Berlichingen was seriously injured in battle and lost his right arm. He is said to have had a metal hand fitted shortly thereafter, which he used to great effect in combat. This metal hand became one of Berlichingen's most famous attributes, and he became known as "Götz of the Iron Hand".

Despite his injury, Berlichingen continued to be active in various wars and conflicts, and was eventually imprisoned by the Holy Roman Emperor, Charles V, for his involvement in a peasant rebellion. He was eventually released and went on to live out the rest of his life as a private citizen, dying in 1562 at the age of 82.

Berlichingen's life and adventures were the subject of numerous poems, plays, and other works of literature, and he remains a famous figure in German history to this day. He is often remembered as a symbol of courage and defiance in the face of adversity, and his metal hand has become a symbol of technological innovation and the human spirit.

THE BIRTH OF MODERN FINANCIAL TRADING

1869

The opening of the Suez Canal in 1869 was a significant event in the history of the global economy. This man-made waterway connected the Mediterranean Sea to the Red Sea, allowing ships to bypass the lengthy and dangerous trip around the southern tip of Africa. The canal reduced the travel time between Europe and Asia, dramatically increasing trade and commerce between the two continents. However, the opening of the canal also led to the birth of modern financial derivatives. As trade between Europe and Asia increased, so did the demand for shipping insurance. Shipping insurance protected merchants against the risk of loss due to accidents or other events that might cause damage to their cargo.

To meet this demand, a group of financiers in London began to trade in derivatives based on the price of shipping insurance. These financial instruments, known as "marine insurance futures," were essentially bets on the future price of shipping insurance. They allowed traders to hedge against the risk of loss due to events such as shipwrecks or piracy, and they soon became popular among merchants and investors alike. However, the early days of marine insurance futures were not without their difficulties. The market was largely unregulated, and many traders engaged in risky behavior, such as leveraging large amounts of debt to make bets on the direction of insurance prices.

Unfortunately, this risky behavior proved to be the downfall of many early traders in marine insurance futures. When the market turned against them, many were unable to meet their obligations, and they faced ruin. The early demise of these traders was a cautionary tale, demonstrating the dangers of speculative behavior in financial markets. Despite these early setbacks, the market for marine insurance futures continued to grow, and it eventually evolved into the modern derivatives market we know today. Today, financial derivatives play a crucial role in the global economy, providing a way for businesses and investors to manage risk and protect against loss. However, the early traders of marine insurance futures serve as a reminder of the need for caution and discipline in financial markets, and the dangers of taking on too much risk.

THE GREATEST BAROQUE COMPOSER

1600s

The story of the greatest Baroque composer never known is a tale that spans over three centuries and continues to this day. It is the story of a musical genius who lived in Salzburg, Austria in the late 1600s, a man who composed some of the most beautiful and sophisticated music of his time, yet whose name has been lost to history.

The search for this composer began in the early 20th century, when musicologists and historians began to uncover a wealth of Baroque music in the archives of Salzburg's monasteries and churches. Among the works they found were a series of musical compositions that stood out for their exceptional beauty and skill.

Despite their musical brilliance, however, the composer of these works remained unknown. No name was attached to the compositions, and there was no record of the composer's life or works in any of the historical documents of the time.

For nearly a century, the identity of this composer remained a mystery. But in the late 20th century, a new generation of musicologists took up the hunt. They scoured old documents and records, looking for any clues that might shed light on the composer's identity.

And finally, in the early 2000s, they made a breakthrough. They discovered a manuscript of music, long forgotten in a Salzburg archive, that was signed by the composer. The signature was barely legible, but with the help of modern imaging technology, the musicologists were able to decipher it: the name of the composer was Johann Anton Riedel.

Johann Anton Riedel was a local composer and church organist in Salzburg, and he lived in the late 17th and early 18th centuries. He composed a large body of religious music, as well as instrumental music and operas, but his works had been largely forgotten over time.

THE MINNESOTA STARVATION STUDY

1945

During World War II, a study known as the Minnesota Starvation Experiment was conducted to understand the effects of starvation on the human body and to develop effective treatments for starvation in war-torn regions. This experiment was conducted by Ancel Keys, a physiologist at the University of Minnesota, and involved 36 healthy, young male conscientious objectors who volunteered to participate in the study.

The subjects were subjected to a controlled diet that gradually reduced their caloric intake over a period of 6 months, until they reached a state of severe malnutrition. The study aimed to simulate the conditions of starvation experienced by prisoners of war and refugees in Europe. The subjects were required to keep detailed food diaries and undergo extensive physical and psychological examinations to document the effects of starvation on the human body.

The results of the study were sobering. The subjects experienced significant weight loss, muscle wasting, weakness, fatigue, and emotional disturbance. They also exhibited decreased heart rate, body temperature, and anemia. Some subjects also developed edema (swelling) due to a buildup of fluid in the body. The study provided valuable information on the physiological and psychological effects of starvation, and the findings were used to develop treatment protocols for starved populations.

The Minnesota Starvation Experiment is considered a landmark study in the field of nutrition and has had lasting impacts on our understanding of starvation and its effects on the human body. However, it is important to note that the study was conducted under rigorous ethical standards and the subjects were carefully monitored and received medical care throughout the study.

THE GOOD FRIDAY EARTHQUAKE IN ALASKA

March 28, 1964

"Good Friday Earthquake" took place in Alaska on March 28, 1964. The earthquake had a magnitude of 9.2 and was the most powerful earthquake ever recorded in North America and the second most powerful in the world.

At 5:36 PM, the ground shook violently for four minutes, causing widespread damage and tsunamis along the Alaskan coast. The earthquake triggered avalanches, mudslides, and massive waves that devastated many towns and villages. The small fishing town of Valdez was hit particularly hard by the tsunamis, with the entire town being destroyed and most of its residents losing their homes and possessions.

The earthquake and resulting tsunamis took 131 lives, making it one of the deadliest earthquakes in American history. The damage from the event was estimated to be around $311 million, which would be over $2.5 billion in today's dollars.

The earthquake also had significant geologic effects, causing the land to sink and rise along the coast and shifting the coastline by as much as 38 feet in some places. It remains one of the best-studied earthquakes and has helped scientists to better understand the dynamics of earthquakes and plate tectonics.

In conclusion, the "Good Friday Earthquake" was a devastating and memorable event in Alaska's history that had significant impacts on both the people and the environment of the region.

THE RISE OF HANGUL AND ITS IMPACT ON KOREAN SOCIETY

1418-1450

King Sejong the Great of Joseon dynasty ruled Korea from 1418 to 1450. King Sejong is revered in Korean history for his many accomplishments, one of which was the creation of the Korean alphabet, known as Hangul.

Prior to the creation of Hangul, the Korean language was primarily written using Chinese characters, which were difficult for the majority of the population to learn and use. This presented a barrier for the common people to participate in government and cultural activities, as literacy was largely limited to the aristocracy who had the resources to study Chinese characters.

King Sejong recognized the importance of making the Korean language accessible to all, and he gathered a group of scholars to develop a new script that was easy to learn and use. The result was the creation of Hangul, which consists of simple, logically organized characters that could be learned and used by anyone, regardless of their social status or education level.

However, the creation of Hangul was not without controversy. The aristocracy, who were well-versed in Chinese characters and had benefited from the exclusivity of their knowledge, were unhappy with the new script. They saw Hangul as a threat to their privileged status, and they opposed its widespread use.

Despite the opposition, King Sejong and his supporters continued to promote Hangul and make it widely available. Over time, it became the dominant script for the Korean language and is still in use today.

King Sejong's creation of Hangul is widely regarded as a landmark event in Korean history and is celebrated as the National Hangul Day on October 9th. King Sejong is remembered as a visionary leader who worked to improve the lives of his people and create a more equal and just society.

THE UNSOLVED MYSTERY OF NYC's TERROR CAMPAIGN

1940-1957

The "Mad Bomber" case was a series of bombing attacks that took place in the New York City area from 1940 to 1957. The bomber was responsible for planting more than 30 bombs in various public places, including movie theaters, libraries, and office buildings, and the attacks generated widespread fear and panic among the public.

The first bombing took place on November 16, 1940, at the Consolidated Edison building in New York City, and over the next several years, the bomber continued to plant bombs in the area. Despite extensive investigations by law enforcement agencies, the bomber was never caught or identified, and the case remains one of the longest and most complex unsolved criminal cases in the history of the United States. The bomber would often include notes with the bombs that contained cryptic messages, such as "Con Ed is unfair," leading investigators to believe that the bombings were motivated by a personal grudge against the Consolidated Edison company. The bomber's messages became increasingly hostile and threatening over time, and by the 1950s, the bombings had generated widespread fear and panic among the public.

In 1956, the New York City police department received a tip from a psychiatrist named James Brussel, who believed that the bomber was a man in his late 50s or early 60s, who had a grudge against Consolidated Edison and suffered from a mental illness. Brussel's profile was based on a psychological analysis of the bomber's notes and actions, and it proved to be remarkably accurate. The police eventually caught the bomber, who turned out to be George Metesky, a former Consolidated Edison employee who had been injured on the job and felt that the company had treated him unfairly. Metesky was arrested and later found to be mentally ill, and he was institutionalized for the rest of his life. The "Mad Bomber" case remains one of the most fascinating and puzzling criminal cases in the history of the United States, and it has been the subject of numerous books, articles, and documentaries over the years. The case is a testament to the persistence and determination of law enforcement agencies, and it serves as a reminder of the far-reaching impact of a single individual's actions, even in a large and complex city like New York.

THE UNSOLVED MYSTERY OF NYC's TERROR CAMPAIGN

1818

James Dalton was a notorious thief and burglar who operated in Britain in the late 18th and early 19th centuries. Despite being arrested and convicted multiple times, Dalton always managed to escape from prison or avoid capture for long periods of time.

In 1818, Dalton was finally caught and sentenced to transportation, a punishment that involved being sent to one of Britain's overseas colonies, usually in the Americas, to serve out a prison term as a laborer. For most convicts, transportation was a harsh and brutal punishment that involved months of cramped and dangerous travel, followed by years of hard labor and abuse at the hands of their colonial masters.

However, James Dalton proved to be an exception to this rule. Rather than being punished, Dalton saw transportation as an opportunity for a new life and a chance to start over. He quickly adapted to life in the colonies, using his wit and cunning to navigate the rough-and-tumble world of early 19th century America.

Despite being watched closely by the authorities, Dalton continued to engage in criminal activity, eventually becoming one of the most successful and feared criminals in the colonies. He became a legend in his own time, with many tales and legends being told about his daring exploits and cunning schemes.

In the end, James Dalton died a wealthy man, having amassed a fortune through his criminal enterprises. Although he was never able to return to Britain, he left behind a legacy of daring and adventure that has continued to inspire generations of people to this day.

THE PIONEER ON CONSERVATION

18th Century

Charles Waterton was a British explorer, naturalist, and conservationist who lived in the late 18th and early 19th centuries. He is considered to be one of the pioneers of modern conservation, as well as one of the most eccentric figures in the history of British natural history.

Waterton was born into a wealthy family and was sent to travel and explore South America as a young man. There, he developed a deep love and appreciation for the natural world, and became especially fascinated with the diverse array of wildlife that he encountered.

Waterton was particularly interested in the preservation of wildlife, and he is credited with being one of the first people to advocate for the protection of endangered species and ecosystems. He is also remembered for his pioneering work in the field of conservation, and for his role in promoting the idea that the natural world should be protected for future generations.

However, Waterton was not just a serious naturalist and conservationist; he was also known for his eccentric behavior and unique personal style. He was known to dress up in animal skins and mimic the calls of different species, and he was often seen walking around his estate on all fours like a wild animal.

Despite his eccentricities, Waterton was highly respected in his day, and he was considered to be a leading authority on South American wildlife and ecosystems. He was also remembered for his many adventures and explorations, which helped to expand the knowledge of the natural world and inspired others to pursue careers in conservation and

Today, Charles Waterton is remembered as one of the greatest conservationists of his time, and his legacy continues to inspire and influence people around the world. He is also remembered for his unique and quirky personality, which adds an additional layer of fascination to his already remarkable story.

UNLOCKING THE SECRETS OF THE VIRGINIA VAULT

1829

The true story of the set of three encrypted notes from the nineteenth century, also known as the Beale Papers, is shrouded in mystery and has been the subject of much speculation and intrigue for over a century.

According to the legend, the Beale Papers were written in 1820 by Thomas Jefferson Beale, who was said to have discovered a rich deposit of gold, silver, and jewels in a secret location in Virginia. Beale wrote three ciphertexts, each of which described the location of the treasure, the type of treasure, and the names of the people who were to receive it. He then entrusted the papers to a friend, who was to hold onto them until a certain date when the treasure would be claimed.

However, Beale never returned to claim the treasure, and the friend eventually passed away without revealing the decrypted information. The papers remained hidden until the late 1800s, when they were discovered and deciphered by a man named James B. Ward. According to Ward, he was able to decode one of the ciphers, which described the type of treasure and the amount of it, but he was never able to decode the other two, which were said to contain the location of the treasure and the names of the recipients.

Despite the intriguing story, many people believe that the Beale Papers are a hoax and that the ciphers have never been truly decrypted. Some have even suggested that Ward invented the whole story as a way to sell copies of the ciphers and make a profit.

Regardless of whether the Beale Papers are genuine or not, they have captured the imagination of people for over a century and remain one of the most famous unsolved cryptograms in history. To this day, there are still people who are attempting to decode the ciphers and find the legendary treasure of Thomas Jefferson Beale.

THE DEVESTATING AND FURIOUS FLOOD OF THE NORTH SEA

1953

The North Sea flood of 1953, was a severe natural disaster that affected the coastal areas of the Netherlands and the United Kingdom. The storm was caused by a combination of high tides, strong winds, and a heavy storm surge, which caused seawater to overflow the low-lying coastal areas. The flood caused widespread damage and loss of life, particularly in the Netherlands, where over 1,800 people were killed and many more were left homeless.

In the UK, the worst-hit areas were the east coast towns of Norfolk and Suffolk, as well as parts of Essex and Kent. The flood caused widespread damage to homes and businesses, as well as disruption to transport and communication networks. In total, over 300 people lost their lives in the UK as a result of the storm.

The North Sea flood of 1953 was a wake-up call for both the Netherlands and the UK, and both countries took steps to improve their coastal defenses and flood-warning systems to prevent similar disasters from happening in the future. Despite these efforts, however, the risk of coastal flooding remains a concern in many parts of the North Sea region, particularly in light of the threat posed by climate change and rising sea levels.

THE EPIC STORY OF A FINNISH SNIPER WHO TOOK 500 SOVIET LIVES

1940

The story of the "White Death" refers to a Finnish sniper named Simo Häyhä, who was a legendary figure in the Winter War between Finland and the Soviet Union during World War II. Häyhä was born on December 17, 1905, in the Finnish municipality of Rautjärvi and was a farmer before the outbreak of the war.

During the Winter War, Häyhä served as a sniper in the Finnish army, and he quickly gained a reputation for his deadly accuracy. He was said to have used a standard Finnish Mosin-Nagant rifle and a simple iron sight, and he was incredibly effective in the winter conditions of the conflict, using his white camouflage to blend in with the snow.

According to reports, Häyhä was credited with killing over 500 Soviet soldiers, making him one of the most successful snipers in military history. His reputation as the "White Death" spread throughout the Soviet army, and soldiers became afraid to venture out in the open for fear of being picked off by the deadly marksman.

After the Winter War ended in March 1940, Häyhä was seriously wounded in a battle and remained in a coma for several days. Although he survived the injury, he suffered from permanent facial disfigurement and was unable to speak for the rest of his life.

Despite his silence, Simo Häyhä remained a national hero in Finland, and he was widely respected for his bravery and skill as a sniper. He lived a quiet life until his death on April 1, 2002, at the age of 96.

The legend of the "White Death" serves as a reminder of the incredible bravery and skill of Finnish soldiers during the Winter War, and of the sacrifices they made in defense of their country.

HOW A PHARMACIST HELPED CHANGE THE FRENCH DIET

18TH CENTURY

The potato was actually introduced to France in the late 16th century and was initially met with resistance due to its unfamiliarity and misconceptions about its nutritional value.

According to the legend, a pharmacist named Antoine-Augustin Parmentier was imprisoned by the Prussians during the Seven Years' War and was forced to subsist on a diet of potatoes. Upon his release, he became a passionate advocate for the crop and is said to have convinced the French to adopt it by hosting elaborate dinners where all of the dishes were made from potatoes, and by staging "potato fields" guarded by soldiers to give the impression that the crop was valuable and worth stealing.

While it is true that Parmentier was a proponent of the potato and worked to promote its cultivation, there is little evidence to support the idea that he staged these elaborate events to trick the French into adopting the crop. Instead, it seems that his efforts, along with those of other advocates, helped to dispel some of the myths and misconceptions surrounding the potato and led to its eventual acceptance as a staple food in France and other parts of Europe.

So, while the story of a pharmacist tricking the French people into adopting the potato may be a charming legend, the truth is that the adoption of the crop was a slow and gradual process, driven by a combination of scientific research and changing attitudes.

THE UNETHICAL MILGRAM EXPERIMENT

1960s

The notorious Milgram experiment, named after psychologist Stanley Milgram. The experiment was conducted at Yale University in the early 1960s and aimed to measure obedience to authority.

In the experiment, participants were told they were taking part in a study about memory and learning and were instructed to deliver electric shocks to another participant (who was actually an actor) whenever they made an error on a memory task. The shocks were staged and increased in severity with each error, with the actor pretending to be in increasing pain and distress.

Despite the fact that the participants could hear the actor's cries of pain, many continued to deliver the shocks at the request of the experimenter, who was dressed in a lab coat and represented authority. The results showed that over 60% of participants delivered the highest voltage shock, even though they believed they were causing severe pain to the actor.

The Milgram experiment has been widely criticized for its unethical methods, as the participants were subjected to significant stress and were not fully informed of the true nature of the experiment. It is now considered unethical by many in the field of psychology and would not be approved by ethical review boards today.

Despite its ethical shortcomings, the Milgram experiment remains one of the most famous and widely cited studies in the history of psychology and continues to be the subject of much debate and discussion.

THE REMARKABLE STORY A JAPANESE FISHERMAN WHO CONQUERED THE NORTH PACIFIC

19TH CENTURY

The story of the Japanese Fishing Boat No. 13 is a remarkable tale of survival and human endurance. In the late 19th century, a group of seven Japanese fishermen set out to sea on a traditional fishing vessel. However, their journey took a dramatic turn when they encountered a powerful storm that swept them off course and into the vast expanse of the North Pacific.

Adrift at sea, the crew faced numerous challenges as they struggled to survive. Their provisions were limited, and they were forced to catch fish and collect rainwater to sustain themselves. The harsh conditions at sea also took a toll on their mental and physical health, as they fought off exposure, fatigue, and despair.

Despite these difficulties, the crew held on to hope and never lost their determination to return home. After many months at sea, their prayers were finally answered when their boat washed up on the shores of what is now Washington State in the United States.

The arrival of the Japanese fishermen caused a stir in the local community, and their story quickly made headlines in the press. The Japanese consul in San Francisco was notified, and he arranged for the return of the sailors to their home country.

The tale of the Japanese Fishing Boat No. 13 serves as a testament to the resilience and perseverance of the human spirit. It is also an important moment in the history of cultural exchange between Japan and the United States, as it marked one of the first recorded encounters between the two nations in modern times.

The story of the ghost ship of the North Pacific continues to be remembered and celebrated, inspiring countless generations with its message of hope and survival against the odds.

THE EPIC JOURNEY OF A BALLOON TO THE NORTH POLE

1897

The three adventurers were Norwegian explorer Fridtjof Nansen, American engineer and balloonist Samuel Lone, and Swedish engineer Nils Strindberg. Nansen was a well-known explorer who had previously attempted to reach the North Pole on foot and by boat. Lone was an experienced balloonist who had made several successful long-distance balloon flights, while Strindberg was a talented engineer who had developed the hydrogen production method used in the expedition.

The team's plan was to launch a hydrogen balloon from the small island of Danskøya in the Arctic Sea and then drift over the polar ice cap, eventually reaching the North Pole. On July 11th, 1897, the three adventurers set off in their balloon, named the "Eagle". The world watched with bated breath as they disappeared into the sky.

However, things did not go as planned. Strong winds separated the balloon from its supporting iceboat and carried it far off course. The adventurers drifted for several days before finally landing on the remote island of Kvitøya in the Svalbard archipelago. Stranded and without proper supplies, Nansen, Lone, and Strindberg faced extreme hardship and danger as they tried to make their way back to civilization.

In the end, the three adventurers were rescued by a whaling ship and eventually returned home. Despite their failure to reach the North Pole, their expedition was still considered a success due to their bravery and the valuable scientific data they collected during their journey.

The story of the three adventurers who tried to reach the North Pole via hydrogen balloon in 1897 is a testament to the human spirit of exploration and the bravery of those who dared to dream and attempt the impossible.

THE QUIRKY WORLD OF NAKED MOLE RATS

1960s

The naked mole rat, also known as the "sand puppy," is a strange and unusual creature that lives underground in the deserts of East Africa. This species of rodent is well-known for its unusual appearance and its ability to survive in extremely harsh conditions.

But what sets the naked mole rat apart from other mammals is its unique biology. Unlike most other mammals, naked mole rats have a highly social and hierarchical society, much like that of ants or bees. The colony is dominated by a single female, known as the "queen," who is responsible for reproducing and maintaining the population.

However, the true nature of naked mole rats was actually predicted long before their behavior was ever observed. In the late 1960s, a researcher named John Jarvis proposed that the naked mole rat's physiology was specifically adapted to its subterranean lifestyle. He predicted that the species would be highly social, with a single dominant female who was responsible for reproducing, and that the colony would rely on a highly organized system of cooperation and division of labor.

Years later, when naked mole rats were finally studied in their natural habitat, scientists were amazed to find that Jarvis's predictions were accurate. The species was indeed highly social, with a single dominant female who controlled reproduction and a highly organized system of cooperation and division of labor. This was a remarkable discovery, as it demonstrated that an animal's biology can be shaped by its environment, and that scientists can make predictions about an animal's behavior based on its physiology.

Today, naked mole rats continue to fascinate scientists and researchers due to their unique biology and ability to survive in such harsh conditions. They have become important models for the study of aging, pain perception, and cancer, as they are one of the few species that are resistant to cancer and can live up to 30 years, much longer than other rodents of their size. The quirky biology of naked mole rats has made them one of the most intriguing species on the planet, and their story is a testament to the power of scientific prediction and discovery.

THE RISE AND FALL OF CHILE'S TECHNOLOGICAL UTOPIA

1970s

In the 1970s, Chile was ruled by President Salvador Allende, who was elected as the first Marxist president in a democratic election in South America. Allende implemented a number of ambitious social and economic reforms aimed at transforming the country into a socialist state. One of the most notable of these initiatives was Project Cybersyn, an ambitious effort to network and automate the country's entire economy.

The project was led by British cyberneticist Stafford Beer, who envisioned a system that would use computer technology to manage the country's economic resources and improve decision-making processes. The project aimed to create a centralized network of computers that would collect data on all aspects of the Chilean economy and use it to optimize the allocation of resources.

Despite initial progress and excitement about the project's potential, political upheaval and the intervention of the CIA eventually put a halt to its progress. As the political situation in Chile became more unstable, the CIA increased its efforts to destabilize the Allende government. In September of 1973, a military coup led by General Augusto Pinochet overthrew Allende, and the new military regime quickly moved to dismantle Project Cybersyn and silence its supporters.

Although Project Cybersyn was ultimately unsuccessful in transforming the Chilean economy, it remains a fascinating example of how technology and political ideals can intersect. The project represents a unique and audacious attempt to use computer technology to build a better society, and it continues to inspire discussions and debates about the potential of technology to shape the future.

In recent years, Project Cybersyn has been the subject of renewed interest, as scholars and technologists have rediscovered its innovative approach to economic planning and its potential lessons for contemporary debates about the role of technology in society.

UNDERSTANDING THE POWER OF SOLAR ERUPTIONS

January 10, 1709

Coronal mass ejections (CMEs) are massive eruptions of plasma and magnetic field from the Sun's corona. The phenomenon was first recorded in the 18th century and has been the subject of extensive scientific study since then.

On 10 January 1709, pioneering weather observer William Derham recorded an event outside his home near London, which is believed to have been a CME. However, it wasn't until the 20th century that scientists were able to study the Sun in detail and understand the nature of CMEs.

CMEs are driven by the Sun's magnetic field and occur when magnetic energy builds up and is suddenly released in the corona. This releases a huge amount of plasma, which travels through space at high speeds and carries with it a magnetic field. When a CME reaches the Earth, it can interact with the Earth's magnetic field, causing a geomagnetic storm.

These geomagnetic storms can have a range of effects on human technology, including power outages, disruptions to communication and navigation systems, and damage to satellites. They can also pose a hazard to astronauts, as the increased radiation can be harmful to human health.

Despite the potential risks posed by CMEs, scientists have made significant progress in understanding and predicting them. By studying the Sun's magnetic field, observing the behavior of CMEs, and using sophisticated computer models, scientists are able to provide early warning of CMEs and take steps to mitigate their effects.

Overall, the history and science of CMEs is a fascinating and ongoing area of research, and the knowledge gained from studying them has helped to improve our understanding of the Sun and its impact on the Earth and our technology.

THE MADNESS OF CLIPPERTON ISLAND

1930

Clipperton Island is a remote coral atoll located in the Eastern Pacific Ocean. It has a long and dark history, including a failed attempt at colonization in the early 20th century and being occupied by Mexican and American forces during World War I. In 1930, a group of seven people, including a French couple and five Polynesian workers, established a colony on the island to harvest guano (bird excrement used as fertilizer). However, the colony soon fell into peril when the only adult man, a worker named Maxime Laopen, became mentally unstable.

Laopen's descent into madness was gradual, but it wasn't long before he became abusive and tyrannical towards the other colonists. He hoarded food and supplies, and subjected the women and children to physical and psychological abuse. The situation on the island became dire, and the colonists were eventually forced to turn to cannibalism to survive. In 1932, a passing ship spotted smoke signals from the island and rescued the survivors, who told their horrific story to the world.

The events that took place on Clipperton Island remain shrouded in mystery to this day, and it's unclear what exactly led Laopen to become so violent and unstable. Some speculate that it may have been a result of isolation and stress, while others believe that he may have suffered from a pre-existing mental illness. Regardless of the cause, the events on Clipperton Island serve as a cautionary tale about the dangers of isolation and the importance of mental health.

THE MURDER OF PRESIDENT CHARLES J. GUITEAU

1881

The assassination of James A. Garfield, the 20th President of the United States, was shot by Charles J. Guiteau on July 2, 1881.

Charles Guiteau was a disgruntled and disturbed man who had failed in various endeavors, including a career as a lawyer and a preacher. He believed that he was entitled to a government job as a reward for his supposed role in Garfield's election, and when his demands were not met, he became fixated on the President.

On July 2, 1881, Guiteau approached President Garfield as he waited for a train at the Baltimore and Potomac Railroad Station in Washington, D.C. Guiteau drew a revolver and fired two shots at the President, one of which struck him in the back. Garfield was taken to the White House, where he clung to life for several weeks before succumbing to his wounds on September 19, 1881.

Guiteau was arrested at the scene of the shooting and was later tried and convicted of assassination. He was hanged on June 30, 1882.

The assassination of James A. Garfield was a shock to the nation and led to a heightened sense of security for future Presidents, including the creation of the U.S. Secret Service, which was originally established to combat the counterfeiting of currency but later became responsible for the protection of the President.

THE TROUBLED FEDEX ENGINEER TOOK CONTROL OF FLIGHT 705

November 29, 1994

FedEx Flight 705 was a scheduled cargo flight from Memphis, Tennessee, to San Jose, California, when a troubled FedEx flight engineer named Auburn Calloway boarded the plane unannounced and attempted to carry out a dangerous plan. Calloway had a history of disciplinary problems and was facing termination from the company, and he believed that he had nothing left to lose.

On the night of the flight, Calloway armed himself with hammers and attempted to gain control of the plane. He confronted the two pilots, but they managed to subdue him and safely land the plane in Memphis.

The incident was widely covered by the media and was seen as a testament to the bravery and resourcefulness of the flight crew. Calloway was arrested and later sentenced to life in prison without the possibility of parole.

The hijacking attempt of FedEx Flight 705 was a terrifying event that brought attention to the issue of workplace stress and its potential consequences. It also served as a reminder of the importance of having proper security measures in place to protect passengers and crew.

THE UNPLANNED AND PROLONGED SKYDIVE THROUGH A THUNDERSTORM

August 29, 1959

Piantanida was a seasoned skydiver who had set a record for the highest parachute jump ever made in the United States. On the day of his fateful jump, he was attempting to break the world record for the highest altitude skydive. He climbed into a helium-filled balloon and ascended to over 40,000 feet, when suddenly, his balloon was enveloped by a severe thunderstorm.

As the storm raged around him, Piantanida was battered by strong winds and lightning, and his oxygen supply was knocked out. Despite these challenges, he managed to freefall for over 40,000 feet before finally deploying his parachute. However, he quickly realized that the severe weather conditions had damaged his parachute, and he began to spin out of control.

Despite his best efforts, Piantanida was unable to regain control of his descent and plummeted to the ground, where he died from his injuries. His death was a shock to the skydiving community, and his story served as a reminder of the dangers and uncertainties associated with extreme skydiving.

The unplanned and prolonged skydive through a thunderstorm made by Nicholas Piantanida remains one of the most memorable moments in skydiving history, and it continues to inspire skydivers and adventurers around the world.

THE ULTIMATE GAME SHOW CON ARTIST

1980s

Michael Larson, a man from Ohio, became obsessed with the game show "Press Your Luck" in the 1980s. He noticed that the show's game board followed a predictable pattern, and he believed he could use this to his advantage.

Larson spent months recording and studying the show, using VCRs to play back episodes and freeze-frame the board. He eventually discovered that the pattern was not completely random, but rather followed a loop of five sequences.

Larson then developed a system to memorize the pattern and time his button presses to stop the board on high-value squares. He auditioned for the show and was selected as a contestant.

During the taping of the show, Larson successfully hacked the game board by hitting the button at the exact right time and won an unprecedented $110,237 in cash and prizes, which at the time was the highest amount ever won on a game show.

Although the producers were suspicious of Larson's win, they eventually determined that he had not broken any rules and paid him his winnings. Larson's story became a legend in the world of game shows and inspired a book and a TV movie about his exploits.

THE RAMPAGE OF THE KILLDOZER

2004

Marvin Heemeyer was a muffler repairman in Granby, Colorado, who became embroiled in a long-standing dispute with local officials over zoning laws and business permits. He believed that the town's government was conspiring against him and his business.

In 2004, Heemeyer took drastic measures to get revenge. He spent over a year modifying a bulldozer with thick metal plates and layers of concrete, turning it into a nearly indestructible tank-like vehicle. On June 4, he drove the bulldozer through town, demolishing the buildings of local officials who he believed had wronged him.

During the rampage, Heemeyer damaged or destroyed 13 buildings, including the town hall, the library, and the local newspaper office. The police were powerless to stop him, as the bulldozer was virtually impervious to their weapons.

The rampage lasted for over two hours before Heemeyer took his own life, either by shooting himself or through a self-inflicted gunshot wound from one of the bulldozer's weapons.

Heemeyer's actions shocked the town and made national news. He had been a reclusive figure, but after the incident, details about his life and motivations were uncovered. Some saw him as a hero who stood up to a corrupt government, while others saw him as a disturbed individual who caused needless destruction.

The bulldozer used by Heemeyer, often referred to as the "Killdozer," has since become a symbol of frustration and revenge. It has been featured in films, television shows, and video games, and is often cited in discussions about mental health and workplace grievances.

THE INFAMOUS PSYCHOLOGICAL EXPERIMENTS ON INFANTS

1920

There are several unethical experiments that have been conducted on infants, but one of the most well-known is the "Little Albert" experiment, conducted by psychologist John B. Watson and his graduate student Rosalie Rayner in 1920.

The experiment aimed to demonstrate that fear could be conditioned in infants by pairing a loud noise with a white rat. They selected a 9-month-old infant named Albert, who was initially unafraid of the rat.

The experiment involved placing the white rat in front of Albert and then making a loud noise by striking a steel bar with a hammer behind his head. This sequence was repeated several times, and eventually, Albert began to cry and display fear whenever he saw the rat, even without the loud noise.

The experimenters also attempted to generalize the fear response to other objects, such as a rabbit, a dog, and a fur coat. Albert's fear response was found to have generalized to some of these objects.

The experiment is considered highly unethical by today's standards, as the infant was subjected to psychological trauma without his or his mother's consent, and the long-term effects on Albert are unknown, as he was never desensitized to his fear.

THE 1985 COCA-COLA REFORMULATION DEBACLE

1985

In 1985, the Coca-Cola Company decided to reformulate their flagship soft drink, Coca-Cola, to compete with the growing popularity of sweeter soft drinks like Pepsi. However, the new formula was met with widespread backlash from consumers who preferred the original taste.

The reaction was outsized because Coca-Cola had become a cultural icon in America and around the world, and people felt a strong emotional attachment to the original taste. This was amplified by the company's marketing campaign, which had positioned the reformulation as a major change that would usher in a new era of the brand.

Despite protests and boycotts, Coca-Cola continued to push the new formula, even as sales plummeted. Finally, after three months, the company reintroduced the original formula under the name "Coca-Cola Classic," which quickly regained its status as the best-selling soft drink in America.

The debacle taught the Coca-Cola Company a valuable lesson about the power of brand loyalty and the importance of listening to consumer feedback. It also demonstrated the enduring influence of the original Coca-Cola formula, which remains a cultural touchstone to this day.

THE TRUE STORY OF NAZI SPIES IN AMERICA

June 1942

During World War II, Nazi Germany sent a number of spies to the United States in an effort to gather intelligence, carry out sabotage, and disrupt the American war effort.

One of the most notable examples was a group of eight German saboteurs who arrived in the United States via submarine in June 1942. They were tasked with destroying strategic targets, such as factories, bridges, and water facilities. However, they were quickly discovered by the FBI and arrested before they could carry out their mission.

Another notable case involved a German-American named William Sebold, who was recruited by the FBI to act as a double agent. Sebold was able to gather valuable information about Nazi spies operating in the United States and helped to thwart their activities.

The Nazi spy effort in America was part of a larger strategy to disrupt the Allied war effort and gain an advantage in the conflict. While some spies were successful in gathering intelligence, the majority was caught by American law enforcement and military personnel, and their efforts to sabotage the war effort were largely unsuccessful.

The story of Nazi spies in America highlights the importance of intelligence gathering and counterespionage in times of war, as well as the risks of foreign interference in national security. It also serves as a reminder of the sacrifices made by those who fought to defend the United States during World War II.

THE MYSTERIOUS DEATHS OF THOUSDANDS OF SHEEP IN SKULL VALLEY, UTAH

1968

In 1968, approximately 3,000 sheep died in Skull Valley, Utah. The incident gained attention when a local farmer, Calvin Brooks, reported that his entire flock of 1,000 sheep had died overnight. Other nearby farmers reported similar losses, with some estimating that up to 6,000 sheep may have died in total.

The cause of the deaths was initially a mystery, and some theories suggested that the sheep had been poisoned by chemical weapons testing at a nearby military base. However, subsequent investigations revealed that the likely cause was exposure to nerve gas released during military testing at the nearby Dugway Proving Ground.

The US Army initially denied responsibility for the incident, but eventually acknowledged that the nerve gas had been released during a test at Dugway. The incident led to increased scrutiny of chemical and biological weapons testing, and prompted reforms to improve safety measures and prevent future incidents.

THE SECRET PNEUMATIC SUBWAY OF NEW YORK CITY'S PAST

19ᵀᴴ CENTURY

In the late 19th century, inventor Alfred Ely Beach built an experimental pneumatic subway in secret beneath Broadway in New York City. The subway consisted of a 312-foot tunnel with a 22-foot diameter, and was powered by a giant fan that pushed a train car through the tunnel at speeds of up to 30 miles per hour.

Beach built the subway in secret because he feared that the city's political establishment would not support his project. However, he was eventually able to open the subway to the public, and it operated for several years as a novelty attraction.

Despite the subway's success, Beach was unable to convince the city government to support his vision for a larger, more comprehensive pneumatic subway system. Instead, the city opted to invest in the more traditional electric subway system that is still in use today. However, Beach's pioneering work in pneumatic transportation paved the way for later innovations in the field.

A TECHNOLOGICAL MARVEL THAT COULDN'T TAKE FLIGHT

1949

The Bristol Brabazon was a large and ambitious airliner designed and built by the Bristol Aeroplane Company in the United Kingdom during the post-World War II period. Named after the famous 18th-century English engineer, John Brabazon, the aircraft was intended to be a symbol of Britain's technological prowess and a key player in the future of commercial aviation.

With a wingspan of 230 feet and a length of 177 feet, the Brabazon was an enormous aircraft for its time. It was designed to carry up to 100 passengers and had a range of 5,000 miles, making it well-suited for long-haul flights. The aircraft was powered by eight Bristol Centaurus radial engines, each capable of producing up to 3,000 horsepower, and featured an innovative pressurized cabin to provide passenger comfort and safety.

The development of the Brabazon, however, was not without its challenges. The aircraft faced numerous technical issues during its design and construction, including problems with the engines, landing gear, and fuel system. These setbacks resulted in significant delays and increased costs, which made the project increasingly difficult to justify from an economic standpoint.

Despite these challenges, the Brabazon made its first flight in 1949, becoming the largest aircraft in the world at that time. It was an impressive feat of engineering, and the aircraft drew crowds wherever it went. The Brabazon's maiden flight was attended by over 40,000 people, and its arrival at the Farnborough Air Show was a highlight of the event.

However, despite its size and technological advancements, the Brabazon was not a commercial success. It was prohibitively expensive to produce and operate, and airlines were hesitant to invest in an untested and costly aircraft. Only one example was ever built, and after a brief period of testing, the Brabazon was retired and scrapped in 1953, marking the end of a promising but ultimately unsuccessful chapter in the history of aviation.

THE POISONOUS CHEMIST WHO FOUGHT TO SAVE THE WORLD

20th century

In the early 20th century, Thomas Midgley was a chemist working for General Motors. He invented two major technological advancements: leaded gasoline and freon, which were widely used in industry and households.

However, Midgley's inventions turned out to have disastrous consequences for the environment and human health. Leaded gasoline caused severe air pollution, while freon contributed to the depletion of the ozone layer.

One of Midgley's inventions, a type of organic mercury compound called "ethylmercury" (also known as "ethyl-mercuric-cresol"), was added to paint as a preservative. This neurotoxin was incredibly harmful and led to numerous cases of mercury poisoning, including cases of Minamata disease in Japan.

In the 1960s, geochemist Clair Patterson discovered that lead from gasoline was contaminating the environment and causing lead poisoning in humans. He also recognized the dangers of ethylmercury and was concerned about the health risks it posed.

Patterson spoke out against the use of leaded gasoline and ethylmercury, but Midgley and the industry he represented were resistant to change. It wasn't until years later that their harmful effects were fully understood and action was taken to regulate and ban them.

Despite his well-intentioned efforts to innovate, Midgley's legacy is a cautionary tale of the unintended consequences of technological advancement and the importance of scientific responsibility.

HOW AN INFECTION LED TO A CURE

October 1, 1890

On October 1st, 1890, William B. Coley, an American surgeon, accidentally discovered a fascinating medical phenomenon that would later become the basis for an innovative cancer treatment. While treating a patient with a severe case of sarcoma, a type of cancer that affects the connective tissue, Coley noticed that the patient's tumors had disappeared after he contracted a severe bacterial infection.

Intrigued by this discovery, Coley began experimenting with the use of bacteria to treat cancer patients. He developed a bacterial mixture, now known as Coley's Toxins, which he injected into cancer patients. The treatment worked by stimulating the immune system to attack cancer cells.

Coley's initial experiments were met with skepticism by the medical community, but he continued to refine his bacterial mixture and successfully treated a number of cancer patients. His work was further validated in the 1930s, when a researcher at the Memorial Sloan Kettering Cancer Center in New York City confirmed the effectiveness of Coley's Toxins in treating cancer.

Today, Coley's Toxins are no longer used in their original form, but his work paved the way for modern immunotherapy treatments for cancer. His discovery of the link between bacterial infections and cancer has also led to a better understanding of the role of the immune system in fighting cancer. William B. Coley's accidental discovery remains a fascinating story of scientific serendipity and persistence in the face of skepticism.

THE UNTOLD STORY OF THE COMMANDOS WHO FOUGHT TO END THE WAR

November 19, 1942

On 19 November 1942, a group of Royal Air Force Halifax bombers conducted a daring mission known as Operation Freshman. The objective was to destroy the heavy water production facilities in Vemork, Norway, which were believed to be critical to Nazi Germany's nuclear weapons program.

The operation involved two Halifax bombers towing gliders carrying a team of commandos who were to land near the facility and destroy it. However, the mission was plagued by bad weather and mechanical problems, and one of the gliders crashed, killing everyone on board.

The survivors of the crash were quickly captured by German forces and executed. The other Halifax bomber was also shot down, and its crew was taken prisoner.

Although the operation was a failure, it highlighted the importance of the heavy water production facilities, and subsequent efforts by the Norwegian resistance and Allied forces eventually led to their destruction, effectively sabotaging Germany's nuclear program. The story of Operation Freshman remains a fascinating and tragic chapter of World War II history.

THE UNTOLD STORY OF THE COMMANDOS WHO FOUGHT TO END THE WAR

November 19, 1942

On 19 November 1942, a group of Royal Air Force Halifax bombers conducted a daring mission known as Operation Freshman. The objective was to destroy the heavy water

www.ingramcontent.com/pod-product-compliance
Lightning Source LLC
Chambersburg PA
CBHW081944160726
47999CB00008B/2502